GATEWAY TO AMERICA

A BUSINESS AND PERSONAL MEMOIR

Tony Horsley

ISBN 979-8-88644-603-6 (Paperback)
ISBN 979-8-88644-604-3 (Digital)

Covenant Books
11661 Hwy 707
Murrells Inlet, SC 29576
www.covenantbooks.com

Jenny, Hope you enjoy
my journey and the wonderful
remembrance of your dad – my
friend Tim. [Page 5 – Para 3]
Ray

Feb 28, 2025.

To my wife Susan who is always by my side
I will love you for ever

To Susan, my wonderful wife, best friend, mother of our two amazing daughters, and Gigi to our seven incredible grandchildren.

Without her love, support, and encouragement, my journey from the UK to the US would have never been documented.

Loving my close-knit family has been the most fulfilling and happiest experience of my life.

Of all the accomplishments I have achieved in a lifetime, my family is what I am most proud of.

Thank you, Roger Fleet, for your encouragement and insistence that I write this book, and to Bill Woods and Fred Senko for their valuable counsel.

Websites, short videos, and documents are included throughout the book supporting the narrative. Several have been converted to QR codes, enabling you to access these while reading.

Just scan the code with your mobile phone: you can view, forward, save, and print documents and watch videos.

CONTENTS

1

The Early Days: At War

In 1939, Europe was the target of the German invasion. Hitler was becoming more powerful by the day, and clearly Great Britain was in his sights. That May, the twenty-eighth to be exact, was my time to arrive on the scene, in the living room of our home in Birmingham, England. Soon thereafter, what became the Second World War eclipsed our country.

The Midlands incorporating the cities of Coventry and Birmingham was and still remains industrial hubs that were, at the time, the principal wartime targets and subject to massive enemy bombings.

The German bombs hit our neighborhood in 1939 and beyond, wreaking devastation on the population. One dropped in our back garden and blew out every window in the house. Nearby our parents' friend Ernesto Piccioni (Birmingham Italian Consulate and my sister, Susan's godfather) had a direct hit on his home; he was away at the time, and his wife and children drowned in their cellar as the water main burst.

As a newborn, the trauma and grief was not understood; all I remember was the daily sanctuary into our cellar when the warning sirens blasted out, and the cigarette smoking of all the adults began!

My father, during the war, served in the Royal Air Force and was responsible for unexploded aerial bomb disposal activities, basically traveling to sites around the country where unexploded ord-

1

nance threatened local populations. His job simply was to defuse them—not a fun or safe occupation. Happily, he survived, and I, as a newborn, was not aware of the dangers he endured.

Today, as I narrate a life of excitement, challenge, adventure, learning, and accomplishment, we are at war again. Yes, a real "Third World War" is being fought in every corner of every nation on this earth. An invisible war named "Pandemic". Now in its third year, the COVID-19 death toll in the USA has exceeded the number of Americans who died in World War II, the Korean and Vietnam Wars combined. Specifically over one million lives have been lost in the USA to COVID. People of all ages wear protective masks and are mandated to distance themselves from all others.

Government-imposed lockdowns worldwide have been initiated to stem the spread of the deadly virus. Early in 2021, a speedily developed vaccine was administered first to health-care teams, the elderly, and on to the younger population.

As the July 2021 Tokyo Olympics were in progress, without any spectators present, a fast-spreading Delta variant was wreaking havoc on populations around the world. There was no clear light at the end of the tunnel. Meanwhile a new pandemic variant emerged—Omicron—which caused continued and rapid infections throughout almost all countries.

Despite all this, initial signs suggest that the administration of vaccines is providing some control of the spread of the virus and less severe COVID symptoms. The February 2022 Beijing Olympics progressed with many safety measurements in place. The economy, coupled with more normal everyday life, gradually is improving. The huge questions are: is this disastrous event really in its final stages, and how and who really caused it in the first place? Perhaps the answers to these questions will be forthcoming and known by the time the final chapter of this book is written.

2

My Parents

My father, William Harry (Bill) Horsley, and mother, Evelyn (Eve), were married in 1932. They were wonderful parents, and both strived and succeeded in providing the very best for my sister, Susan, and me. We lived in a nice suburb, Kings Heath, on the south side of Birmingham, in a very comfortable three-story house. My mother did not work but rather managed the family affairs and provided a secure and loving environment for all of us. She was a great cook, with her specialty being fried liver and onions. Her secret was that you must never overcook the liver—apply a little flour, fry for a very short time; it was always tender and delicious!

Bill Horsley was quite entrepreneurial and was employed in the design and construction business and established several patents covering suspended ceiling installation and other advanced and unique construction methods.

He was recognized as an inventor, and being an avid golfer, he developed an at-home putting device called The Hole In One. He introduced and launched this product on a UK television show called *Inventors Club*. It was a great success; the product exactly replicated a putting cup (above ground) and could be used within a home (with a low-pile carpet) or outside, on a backyard putting green.

They were great ballroom dancers, often competing in contests and winning many awards and cups. They firmly believed in the best education for my sister and me and, at considerable expense, sent us both to wonderful private boarding schools. The education experience was great for us both, and there is no question that living at a remote school away from home does teach one independence and the ability of self-survival!

Our father passed away in 1960; I was at his side. It was a great loss for all of us. Our mother, though saddened, was very brave and strong. Sister Susan and I were very close with her, and later after we had both immigrated to the United States, she joined us, and we all enjoyed many more years of love and companionship. She never remarried. Quite recently, my daughter Holly, after having three boys, gave birth to a beautiful daughter; she named her Evelyn, after my mother. She is, at this time, three years old and has all my mother's characteristics: nose, mouth, eyes, and spectacular blond curly hair, *plus* her beauty. See pictures in middle of book.

3

Wolverley, England: Sebright School

Eventually the war ended, Hitler was gone, and normal living was reinstated. My sister, Susan, joined the family, and we grew up together—me going to Sebright, a boy's boarding school in Wolverley, near Kidderminster, and she at a boarding school in Bristol. The country was at peace, and our lives were somewhat back to normal!

Wolverley, rural and somewhat isolated was a good experience, a small school that also supported a military cadet force that I participated in. Alex Flint, our French master, was the commanding officer. There were several separate houses, mine being Stanley Baldwin House (named after First Earl Baldwin of Bewdley); though our classes were centralized. The headmaster was Mr. Henniker Gottley.

The most enjoyable activity was my participation in our rugby team. Rugby was my sport, and as captain of our team, we enjoyed considerable success playing against other private schools in the Midlands. We even graduated to seven-a-side rugby and competed in Twickenham, London. With seven players on each team instead of the usual fifteen, it was a fast-running game! My dear friend Tim Leach played against us; he was my oldest friend and lived very close to us in Birmingham. We have remained close friends to this day.

During school holidays, I worked at the Birmingham Accident Hospital as a medical orderly. Essentially my job was to attend to injured patients arriving in ambulances and transmit deceased patients from the wards to the hospital morgue. Both tasks were emotionally challenging; most all the ambulance patients were the results of motorbike accidents. (As a result, I have never ridden a motorbike!)

Transferring deceased patients was tough also; to get from the hospital wards to the morgue, one had to exit the building and go down a long and steep unlit incline adjacent to a river canal. On one occasion, I was called to a ward to move a deceased patient to the morgue. We got the body on my wheeled stretcher, and I proceeded to the morgue. As I started down the canal path, the body sat up, and in terror, I released the stretcher; it went hurtling down toward the morgue and miraculously did not run into the canal. Of course, the "body" was one of my coworkers playing a prank; he almost drowned and could have suffered major injuries in the process!

When Sebright boarding school was concluding, I had the choice of going to university or participating in what was then a mandatory two years of military national service. You could go to university first and then national service, or the other way around. Your choice, but there was no option to be exempt from national service. Meanwhile, I had been communicating with a recruiter with ICI (Imperial Chemical Industries), a large and significant chemical and coatings corporation. His recommendation was to "join the army," gain an officer's commission, then attend university, and subsequently join ICI.

4

Budbrooke Barracks,
Worcestershire, England,
and Malaya–British Army

I followed his recommendation, joined the Royal Warwickshire Regiment in 1958, and began my sixteen weeks of basic training. At its conclusion, I was offered the option of going to officer cadet school (following which I would join the battalion in Northern Ireland) or be transferred to the Sherwood Foresters Regiment and embark on a month-long ocean trip to Malaya to engage in active service, tracking down and fighting the Malayan People's Anti-Japanese Army. I chose the latter; it seemed, at the time, a more exciting opportunity and venture!

When the HMS *Dilwara* headed from Southampton to Singapore, joining the First Battalion—the Sherwood Foresters, there was an intense occupation onboard establishing military operational roles once we, the Sherwood Foresters Battalion, disembarked. When it became known that I had worked in an accident hospital, my future position as a medical orderly was quickly established!

Upon arrival, the troops headed for the "sins" of Singapore, and Monday mornings at the medical center, the penicillin injections were working overtime! We handed out free contraceptives that were hardly ever used!

At this point, I was a private working under Dr. Captain Peter Bewes, together with a medical sergeant and a medical corporal. A total of four medics, including me. Problem was that there were four companies, and within a week, all four were widely separated into different parts of the Malayan jungle. I went to Sungai Siput, a small northern town located deep in the jungle. Each company established their independent and separate base of operations. In simple terms I was the Charlie Company doctor, and everybody accepted me as such and relied on me for their sound medical health!

Yes, I could apply Band-Aids, inject penicillin, and perform minor medical treatments; however, by the third night, I had treated three snake-bite injuries and a neighboring Australian soldier who had been hit on the head with a beer bottle by a drunken comrade. My mother taught me how to sew on a button, but an open-skull wound required more skill. I sewed him up, no anesthetic required; he was so drunk. I fear he was scarred for life!

After six months in the jungle chasing anti-Japanese Army enemies, I determined that I might have been wiser to have chosen to go to officer cadet school back in the UK! I approached this notion with my commanding officer, and to my surprise, he agreed and promised to send me back to the UK to accomplish this.

I was flown back to the UK, passed the War Office Selection Board, and was admitted to Mons Officer Cadet Academy in Aldershot in 1959. Back to normal military life. One big difference and advantage that I enjoyed was that all the cadets I was training with were recent army entrants with no active-duty experience. Whereas I had been fighting a real enemy on the front line in the jungles of Malaya and wore a medal on my dress uniform and insignia on my everyday military garb to prove it! It provided me with a "compelling competitive advantage," something that I learned in the years ahead was a distinctive and valuable asset!

Becoming a second lieutenant in the Sherwood Foresters Infantry Division in 1960, I was transferred to their headquarters in Derby, where I completed my two years national service. It was here that I met a fellow officer who became a lifelong close friend; his name was Tony Dixon. We were two impatient officers completing our national service and anxious to go to work in the real world. We have remained close friends all these years until his recent passing in August 2021. He and his wife, Yvonne, had also moved to the USA and lived nearby in Atlanta.

5

Slough, Buckinghamshire, England: Imperial Chemical Industries

During the period in Derby, I communicated with the ICI personnel manager in Slough, England, whom I had previously been in contact with. His recommendation was that having served in the military and gained a commission, I should skip university, and he hired me on the spot as a marketing trainee at the ICI Paints Division headquarters in Slough, beginning in the fall of 1960.

Slough was a dull city, but close by was Windsor, with a magnificent castle and where many aspects of royalty existed. Early in my ICI training, I met up with Martin Hoad, who, like myself, was a bachelor with a roaming eye for attractive young ladies! We became good friends and together rented a flat in the upper floor of a large house in Windsor, named Ashstead House. Mrs. Leffler owned it and lived on the first level. It was amazing that she put up with us for so many years!

Close by was a wonderful pub—The Windsor Castle—often referred to as "the first and last" because it was located just inside the boundary line of Windsor, had a direct view of the castle, and was the first pub entering Windsor and the last as you left! It was just a three-minute walk from our flat. The owners, Fred and Joy, quickly became close friends as we rapidly became frequent visitors.

Our parties became well known and well attended; the format was simple: our guests were directed to the Windsor Castle pub before arriving at our flat, the invitations were scripted as shown below, and the all-night events quickly became famous from participants as far away as London.

O'er hill and dale, the tocsin rings,
Heralding a night of frolicsome things.
To Royal Windsor wend your way,
On Saturday eve, the 6 of May.
Seek the "Windsor Castle", enter here,
To ask your way and enjoy good beer.
At closing time, as the candles flicker,
Arm yourself with a bottle of liquor.
At "Ashtead House" will end your quest,
For your to be an honored guest.

One other noteworthy aspect of our flat was that to commute to work at our ICI office in Slough, we had to drive through the town of Eton and down Eton High Street. This took us past Eton College, internationally described as "the school for the country's most powerful and privileged." All students wore formal dress—top hats and tails! Many future British prime ministers attended, including British PM, Boris Johnson. It was quite a scene and very unique.

Martin and I created a decorating business and, in the evenings and weekends, painted houses around Windsor. We largely used the profits to purchase classic older cars to upgrade and sell. The first was an SS-type Jaguar, a fine vehicle, which developed a loose-fitting front wheel. We fixed this by wrapping sacking around the axle and tightening the locking nut. This was not a reliable solution; we sold the car, and shortly after the transaction, we noticed traffic backing up, leading toward Windsor Castle. We followed the trail and quickly discovered the car—minus one wheel—blocking traffic in both directions.

We recruited a couple more bachelors to move into the flat: Tony Pinnegar and Quinten Clough. We had four bedrooms and a huge kitchen/living area. The partying continued at a hectic pace until Martin was promoted to the ICI Millbank office in London, and I to the Birmingham Midland office as a field sales representative in 1964, some two years after joining the company. An easy move. Back home, my father had recently passed away after a short battle with cancer; my mother was happy to have me back.

This was my first experience in direct sales, and it was challenging and fun. I knew from day one that selling would become a lifelong passion and an exciting, rewarding career. No question that my two years in the military gave me the confidence and wherewithal to succeed in this field.

Concurrent with my new sales position, I joined the Royal Warwickshire Territorial Army that was headquartered nearby in Coventry. The TA, its abbreviation, is like the US Reserve Army and is best described as a "part-time volunteer force of the British Army." Sometimes referred to as Saturday-night soldiers. I had risen to the rank of captain upon joining, and for seven years (up until I immigrated to the USA), I participated fully in the training and military events, which included a two-week camp each year, most often in a foreign country.

One is paid for this service, which essentially takes place during evenings and weekends; plus by law, your employer must allow for time off with pay for the annual camps. It was a wonderful experience, great people to soldier with, and yes, the social side was awesome! After my seventh year, I immigrated to the United States and must admit that I really missed the friends and military events I had so enjoyed.

6

Warwickshire, England: Becoming a Salesman

At school and in the armed forces, I always had an eye on commerce, be it repairing fountain pens and reselling them to classmates or creating and selling military artifacts and memorabilia. Selling used cars in Windsor also proved to be a worthwhile business, though not too profitable! At ICI, a big advantage seemed to be that I was not married (as were most of my peers) and thus had the freedom and ability to travel and get involved in any type of sales or marketing endeavor, be it leading a new product market test in the Isle of Man or heading up and managing ICI's entry into the wallpaper business. More details later!

My initial sales territory incorporated the county of Warwickshire, a largely picturesque area to the south of Birmingham. My sales activity and training were directed by the two sales managers, Doug Lockhart and Max Harris, who took me to meet with retailers and distributors of our Dulux paints in my territory, the strongest and most recognized paint brand in the country. This was not a challenge working under their experienced and professional umbrella; however, after two weeks, they determined I was ready to go it alone—time to get nervous!

Entering a retail paint shop, asking for the owner and introducing myself as their new representative was initially scary, even at age twenty-five. Once again, my national service army experience came to the rescue and provided me with a valuable point of reference and maturity. In Great Britain, conscription, as it was called, ended in 1960, shortly after I was discharged from the army.

With the sales training behind me, I realized that the acquisition of *new* accounts was the best road map to growth and success in any business. Better yet, visibility by the company's hierarchy was a plus! The ICI Midland sales director, Harold Drennan, lived in a small and picturesque town called Wootton Wawen (just north of Stratford-upon-Avon).

I determined that securing a new ICI paint retailer close to his home would get his attention! Problem turned out to be that this small village had very few shops, and the largest and most progressive was a grocery store—not the most suitable outlet for paint! Nevertheless, I proceeded and met with the grocery store owner; to my surprise, he was amenable to the idea of stocking a small assortment of Dulux interior paints. Soon his storefront included an inviting display of our products. And yes, Harold Drennan was delighted to see his products in his local store! No question that some of the future outside-the-box projects I was assigned to were a direct result of this initiative!

In 1964, ICI developed a new thixotropic coating that, unlike conventional paints, was very thick in the can and spread easily when applied. At the time, it was a unique technology, which added significantly to the ease of paint application and the quality of the finished appearance. The product needed field testing but in a market that was invisible to competition.

The Isle of Man is a desolate self-governing British Crown Dependency in the Irish Sea between Britain and Northern Island. It is famed for just two things: the annual Manx Grand Prix and Classic TT motorcycle races, held in September each year, and the Manx cat, a breed of domestic cat originating on the Isle of Man, with a naturally occurring mutation that shortens the tail. We determined that no paint competitor would ever visit this remote island or hear of our top secret product tests!

I was directed to go to the island and sell this new and unique product to as many paint retailers as there existed and set up a supporting advertising campaign. The campaign worked, the paint sold well, and our market research satisfied the plans to launch the product nationally throughout the UK.

7

Wallcoverings

A departure from paint was a wallcovering product called Vymura. ICI owned another division called ICI Leathercloth. An offshoot of this business was an artificial leather look-alike wallpaper that was branded Vymura. The Leathercloth division had no interest in this product, and so the manufacturing plant and an excellent team of designers were transferred to the ICI paints division.

The nature of this business was quite different from paint; the product was offered in wallpaper-pattern book collections and sold to retail stores through wallpaper distributors who, for the most part, were not interested in the paint business! I became directly involved in managing this acquisition, which we were able to support with our existing national team of ICI paint sales reps. The business flourished and encouraged ICI management to jump deeper into wallcoverings.

The next acquisition, some six months later, was Withins Wallpaper Mill in Yorkshire. The owner, Ernie Greenshaw, was a delightful Yorkshireman who took the time to teach me the rudiments and intricacies of this business—all of which were quite different from paint!

Looking back over the years to this event, I will define the role and position that wallpaper has represented in the do-it-yourself marketplace, worldwide but particularly in North America, during the last fifty or so years. Having been associated with paint and wallpaper, essentially throughout my career, I will identify the significant product and marketing differences between the two.

Both are designed to cover walls and sometimes ceilings, creating decorative value. There is more skill required to install wallpaper, and it is generally more expensive to buy than paint, particularly when factored on a cost-per-square-foot basis. The real difference lies in their journey to market or how the consumer, contractor, or specifier procures the product.

Paint is simple! It's manufactured in large batches up to five thousand gallons at a time, packaged in pint/quart/gallon and five-gallon containers. It can be precolored or produced as a tint base, in which case the retailer will tint the color in store to that selected by the customer. Application to walls, ceilings, and trim is relatively easy using a brush or roller! Wallpaper is a different animal! The production process is more complex and certainly more capital intensive.

The wallcovering industry has been around for a long time, from back in the early part of the century when surface-print wallpaper was widely produced. Batch numbers were required for each production, and necessary because there could be color inconsistences between each production run of the same pattern (design). In addition, the machinery was and always has been more expensive than a paint mixer!

In the early 1900s, wallpaper was very popular, particularly in Europe, and it largely remains so today. Nevertheless, it has always been a more difficult product to install than paint; however, on the plus side, wallpaper has more than color to offer—design, texture, and multiple colorations exist.

On the minus side, come time to redecorate, existing wallpaper most always needs to be removed; whereas with paint, just apply one or two coats of your new color over the existing one, and you are set!

One other difference is cleanability. Many paints, especially those designed for kitchen and bathrooms, are very tough and can be washed time and time again. Some wallpapers are coated and can be used in kitchen and bath areas and are able to be lightly cleaned with soap and water.

Bottom line is that if you really want to change the character of a room and create a dramatic decor experience, wallpaper will be your best option!

Historically the removal of old wallpaper prior to redecoration can be a tough job! Thankfully some of the newer products are easier with peelable and strippable substrates (base paper). A growing and popular product is peel-and-stick wallpapers that, if removed carefully, can even be reused!

It is important to add that there is a growing market for digitally printed wallcoverings which, in chapter 27, "Distinctive Wallcoverings and Decor," this topic is covered in detail. The bottom line is that while paint is less expensive and easier to use, wallpaper will most often create a more vibrant, different, and exciting decor experience for the homeowner or commercial user.

8

Birdingbury, Warwickshire, England: Graham Heath

During this period with ICI, while living in Birmingham, the hub of my business and customer base was in Coventry, some fifty miles to the south. It was during this time that I reconnected with a very good friend that I had met in the army, Graham Heath. Though born into wealth (his father owned Coventry Radiator Company), he was unspoiled and did not flaunt his position in life.

Graham was well connected, owned racing cars, and was a member of the Cowes Yacht Club on the Isle of Wight, where he moored his magnificent sailing ketch, *Zebedee*. He introduced me to a new side of life, and on one visit to the club, we were at a party in the presence of Prince Philip, the Duke of Edinburgh.

Graham also was in the Territorial Army and, like me, had no shortage of female companions! We would meet for lunch every couple of weeks, and one day, when calling Coventry Radiator to confirm a date, I was routed to a secretary who announced that he had been driving his Lamborghini at excessive speed the day before, flipped the car, and had died. I was devastated, attended the funeral service in Coventry Cathedral, and, after, was invited to join the family at their country estate, The Old Rectory in Birdingbury, not too far from Coventry. It was a very sad event; the immediate family consisted of Mr. and Mrs. Heath, their older son, Brian (who lived away from home), and Nurse, a live-in nanny since the birth of the two boys.

Less than a month later, Graham's father, Harold Heath, was grouse hunting and had a massive heart attack, killing him instantly. Back at the cathedral and at the Old Rectory, Mrs. Heath was beyond distraught. Brian was living in the south of England working for Cooper Tire, so it was up to Nurse to share and nurture her grief.

At this point in my business, Coventry had become the focus of my sales effort, managing retail customers and a distributor who was purchasing annually over £2,000,000 of our paint products—A. R. and W. Cleaver Ltd. I offered to stop by each Thursday evening after work to visit Mrs. Heath and Nurse. Shortly thereafter, I was invited to stay overnight. For the next two years, every Thursday after work in Coventry, I stayed at their home.

The routine was a wonderful respite for them. I would take Mandy, their Lab, for a long walk on the estate, meet with Hales, the gardener, have dinner with Mrs. Heath and Nurse, and spend wonderful evenings talking about Harold and Graham and their many life achievements. I believe this gave them comfort and helped to minimize the huge loss of a son and a husband.

Following my immigration to the USA in 1968, we kept in touch by mail, and shortly after our marriage, Sue and I visited them both in the UK at their new home in Eastbourne on the south coast. Lots of tears but a happy reunion.

9

Atlanta, Georgia, USA

My sister Susan, living in the UK, met the man of her dreams—
another Tony! He was a skilled toolmaker working in Birmingham,
England. A few months after they met, he was recruited by an industrial company called Metals Engineering, located in Greeneville,
East Tennessee, USA.

He left the UK with the promise that he would return to marry
sister Susan following the expiration of his contract. He loved the job
and the location, so instead, my sister emigrated, joined him, and
they were married—unfortunately without my mother or me being
able to be present. Sue also fell in love with East Tennessee, and in
the spring of 1965, they invited me to visit.

I had recently bought a small property on Great Exuma Island
in the Bahamas, while in the UK, so was able to combine a trip to
both places. First stop was Greeneville, Tennessee.

This is a picturesque town in the foothills of the Smokey
Mountains, so I could understand their love of the place. At the end
of the first week, I borrowed Sue's car and drove myself to Knoxville,
the closest town of consequence. Parked the car and strolled down
the High Street. Halfway down, I saw this huge sign hanging over
the sidewalk, announcing, "Snelling & Snelling—Employment
Counselors."

What the heck, I thought, *let's see what they have to offer!* I entered
and met a Jerry Viles, told him I was visiting the US and worked in

the UK coatings business. He quickly proposed my consideration of employment through his network and asked where I would like to interview companies.

The huge map on his wall identified Atlanta as the closest major metro area, so this became my choice. He promised to set up interviews with several paint companies the following week.

I drove down to this huge city the next week, met with three small paint manufacturers, and then with Glidden, a major national coatings company.

First, I met with Jerry Mitchell, the Atlanta district center manager, who passed me on to the southeast regional sales manager, Don Reilly. He interviewed me and moved me on to the regional personnel manager, Jim Lanier, and finally I met with the SE regional director, Jim Beauchamp. He was the lead manager of Glidden's SE division.

His office was huge, and as we began our discussions, he pulled out a pipe and began filling it with tobacco—a welcome sight as I, also at the time, was an avid pipe smoker! I pulled out my pipe and proceeded to follow suit.

The interview was very positive. I was coming from a major UK coatings manufacturer, seeking employment in Atlanta, and he welcomed the opportunity to hire someone who might well add value and differentiation to his sales team. He concluded the meeting by saying, "Horse"—he adopted this name for me—"go back to the UK, get your green card—let us know if you need any help—and we will have a sales position waiting for you as soon as you can return."

Following the very productive trip to Atlanta, I continued my journey to Great Exuma island, flying from Miami, connecting through Nassau. It was a wonderful experience, and I later wrote a short article for the developer's magazine, *Bahama Soundings*, published in June 1965.

One notable event: on the island, I stayed at the Club Peace & Plenty in Georgetown, and at dinner the first night, there were twelve of us dining together; we had been shark fishing earlier. It was May 25, 1965, and that evening, there was a world championship boxing fight between Mohammad Ali and Sonny Liston. We agreed to watch it on TV, and beforehand, we placed in a hat numbered slips of paper, 1–12. Each of us deposited $10 and drew a number that represented the round the fight would end in. I got number 1—no way I thought I could win!

I did *win*! Ali KO'd Liston in the first round. The commentator, excited and confused, called it an "anchor punch." To this day, you can watch the event by googling "Mohammad Ali KO's Liston in first round."

Later, after I was married, I took my wife to Great Exuma. I sold the lot for $40,000 in 2010, a $39,000 profit, thanks to the arrival of a Four Seasons Resort just a couple of miles away! During this trip, we met Wolfgang and Ursula Pohle, a delightful couple from Switzerland. We became good friends and remain so to this day.

I can't say that my objective during my visit to the USA was to seek employment. I had a good job and comfort level in the UK, but somehow this opportunity appealed to me and was challenging. Also I found Atlanta to be a vibrant and exciting city!

I was motivated and excited! I returned to the UK and first consulted with my mother, who I believed might not be happy with the prospect of her second child leaving for a faraway country! She was, however, very positive and encouraged me to seize the opportunity. I will always love and respect her for this support.

On April 1, 1968, I left the UK with my green card in hand and immigrated to the United States. Atlanta was my destination, and I spent the first few days at the home of my sister's friends, during which time I found an apartment to live in. Three guys seeking a fourth in a four-bedroom town house on Shallowford Road became my first US home.

With a salary of $9K a year, I had to purchase a car and feed and house myself! A brand-new teal-green Plymouth Barracuda hatchback was my first purchase, $0 down! This was a hot car and a woman grabber! I thought if only my buddies in the UK could see me now!

Each day, I reported to the Glidden downtown, Luckie Street store at 7:00 a.m. The paint contractors were already in line or at breakfast in an adjacent greasy spoon! I would help tint five-gallon buckets of paint and then learn the characteristics of the various coatings I was about to sell—Spred Satin Interior Latex Wall Paint being our lead brand.

The plan was for me to take over the North Georgia territory from a salesman about to retire; his name was Otis Norton.

Otis was a wonderful person who chewed on an extinguished cigar most of the day. He was happy to be retiring and relished the prospect of delivering all his customers to me. In his car, we drove throughout North Georgia as he introduced me to his customers in Ellijay, Toccoa, Hiawassee, and other remote small towns.

This experience just did not compare to the big-city accounts I had managed in the UK. The customers loved Otis; they embraced me as his replacement and seemed inspired by my British background. One customer insisted on calling me Winston (Churchill) and did so for as long as I was his sales rep!

These sales calls were somewhat nerve-racking for me because Otis rarely discussed the paint business! He inquired after family and personal activities yet *never* asked for a paint order! Don't be concerned, he told me, the orders will follow our visit automatically. I must admit that they often did!

My transition to his territory was competed, and I was on my own. Unhappily Otis passed away some two weeks later. I was invited to his life celebration at HM Patterson Funeral Home. This was a first for me in the USA, and I was astounded upon arrival to witness a full-scale party event in progress. Otis was there in his coffin, fully open, and dressed in his best Sunday suit, together with cigar. He looked magnificent!

A sad occasion, and now I had to move forward and develop a meaningful business within his territory that I had inherited. The total annual sales volume that I was responsible for was a mere $92,000. This number based on my past UK experience was totally inadequate! How in the world could they pay me $9,000 a year plus expenses for such a small-volume sales territory?

I posed this question to my manager, Jerry Mitchell, and he did not seem to share my concern. I therefore challenged him, saying that I was going to conduct an in-depth analysis of the Atlanta and North Georgia retail paint market in order to formulate an action plan. One designed to identify the paint retailers necessary for us to sell to better support my long-term compensation and expense levels.

The next several days, I devoted my time to visiting every single paint retailer listed in the phone/yellow pages in Atlanta and surrounding areas in order to gauge their strength and participation in paint retailing. Happily there was one dominant retail force!

I met again with my immediate boss, Jerry Mitchell, and announced that I had clearly identified the dominant paint retailer in Atlanta and that they were the one and only retail opportunity we should pursue.

"And who would that be?" he asked.

I replied, "Sears."

There was a deadly silence.

He cleared his throat and said, "Not possible. Sears has its own paint manufacturing plants, De Soto Paint, whose factories produce decorative coatings exclusively for Sears retail stores throughout North America! They have a market share that is significantly greater than that of Glidden!"

I was not discouraged with this information and responded that the strength of Glidden's brand awareness was very significant and outperformed that of De Soto! He did not agree and directed me to *not* pursue Sears!

The Sears southeastern headquarters was in a massive headquarters building on Ponce De Leon Avenue that was formally the City of Atlanta Headquarters. The next morning, I called their office and asked to speak to the Sears president or chief executive of operations.

I was put through to a secretary and asked the same question. There was a brief silence, and she said, "His name is Mr. Dean Swift. I will put you through." I was connected directly to Mr. Swift the CEO—he was the man! I then proceeded to fire questions regarding his and our paint market share and brand dominance in the USA and how a partnership between Glidden and Sears could create a significant market force. Again, another silence.

"Your name is Tony, British, right?"

"Yes, sir."

Silence again on the phone! "I can meet you tomorrow morning in my office at 9:00 a.m. Is this okay?"

I replied, "Yes, sir. I will be there."

I arrived on time and was led into a huge office and met with Dean Swift the Sears Southern regional president. He was a most delightful gentleman. We spent some time discussing the challenges and intricacies of the coatings business, and he asked me to identify the UK retail paint characteristics of this business.

We discussed ICI (UK), Glidden, and De Soto, and he explained their long-term paint marketing strategy. He detailed in positive and polite terms that an alliance between Glidden and Sears would be a most unlikely event. Bottom line, Jerry Mitchell had been correct; this was a tough sell! I reported details of the meeting to Jerry following the meeting; he was not happy that I had made the call!

Two days later, he beckoned me into his office and presented me with a plane ticket to Cleveland.

"What is this for?" I asked.

He responded, "I told the top guys at Glidden that I have a crazy Englishman in my midst trying to sell our paints to Sears. They want to meet that crazy person!"

10

Cleveland, Ohio: Glidden Headquarters

"So tell us about your meeting with Sears," was the first question asked by Gary Bechtel (general manager, trade sales) and John Dumble (national dealer sales manager), the two senior executives who ran the Glidden decorative coatings business nationally, from the Cleveland headquarters.

This seemed to me like a trick question or, at best, an adversarial one!

I responded, "No salesman worth his salt can ever survive on a territorial volume of less than a million dollars. Your people hired me to manage a $100,000 business. This makes no sense to me. The retail customer mix in my territory is pathetic. We need to sell larger retailers, preferably multiple-chain store operations that are constantly adding store count."

I then reiterated, "We need to sell *new* business. Sears seemed to me to be an ideal candidate. If because of their paint manufacturing capability, they are off-limits, then we need to seek retail chains that are *not* off-limits!"

More silence; these two guys looked at each other.

"We agree!" They continued, "There is one other issue that has to be addressed. Glidden consists of geographical sales regions— Eastern, Central, Midwest, Southeast, Southwest, Western, and

Canada. Each region is independently managed by a regional director. Each region is financially accountable, and they are also responsible for their sales strategies and new-account growth initiatives."

"This last point is becoming a real challenge because many of the larger retail chain operations are beginning to expand their footprint into multiple markets and, in the process, are crossing our regional boundaries. This is fast becoming difficult to control. We need to appoint a national account manager to take on this responsibility. We think you will fit the bill very well. Are you ready to move to Cleveland?"

*****

Back in Atlanta, I packed my bags and prepared for my northbound trip on July 1, 1969. My brother-in-law, Tony, had recently resigned from his position at Metals Engineering and had moved down to Atlanta with my sister and their two daughters in order to start his own manufacturing business.

I should inject at this point that the entrepreneurial spirit in the USA was and still is tremendously significant; many of those employed in industry are motivated to own their own business, and for the most part, success is highly prevalent! When they made this move, my sister and I encouraged our mother to sell the family home in Birmingham and immigrate to Atlanta. She was seventy years old and loved the idea. There was plenty of room in the Lullwater Road house that I had previously purchased early in 1969. In 1971, she arrived in Atlanta, and our whole family was happily united!

The challenge was that Mother and sister were relocating to Atlanta, and I was moving up to Cleveland. The good news was that in my new position of national account manager, I would be traveling throughout the country and could easily spend weekends in Atlanta!

The national account manager position became a very exciting business, particularly with the emergence of some powerful retail DIY chains across the country: Daylin on the West Coast; Pergament, Channell, and Hechinger in the East; Lowe's and Scotties in the

South; Forest City and Handy Andy in the North. Well-managed businesses driven by seasoned entrepreneurs. (But look out, Home Depot had not yet arrived on the scene!)

A new wave of discount mass-retail paint chains morphed from an unusual source—the department stores segment. The first of which was Dayton Hudson, a Midwest high-end department store chain headquartered in Minneapolis. They saw future weakness in their upscale department store marketing and decided to launch a discount store chain. They named it Target; a bull's-eye was their logo, same as it is today! The store product mix was focused on fashion, clothing, furnishings, hardware, paint/DIY, and later, food and automotive. Simply speaking, the product mix is best described as general merchandise.

Other department stores jumped on the bandwagon: The May Company (St. Louis) with Venture, Rich's (Atlanta) with Richway, and JCPenney (Dallas), to name a few.

There were also some very significant general merchandise chains who sold just about everything: S. S. Kresge (Detroit), who transformed into Kmart, becoming the largest retailer in the USA.

We originally sold S. S. Kresge, a nationwide discount variety store chain, who was renamed the Kmart Corporation in 1977. John Dumble, my boss, personally handled the account, deciding to turn it over to me when I became his national account manager.

We traveled together to their fortlike office complex in Detroit to meet with their paint and decor buyer, Harry Hardisty. Mr. Hardisty, as he was addressed by all, was formal to a tee. He was immaculately dressed and always wore a bow tie.

At the beginning of our sales call, John announced that in the future, I would be handling the Kmart account. I handed Mr. Hardisty my business card, and he produced his Rolodex, removed John's card, and ceremonially dropped it into a large trash can beside his desk, adding mine! Not a word, not a smile—John was history!

Sears, back in 1969, was the largest retailer in the world! In November 2004, Kmart purchased Sears, creating a new identity called Sears Holdings Company. By 2018, they were struggling to survive and filed for bankruptcy. Facing off against Walmart, founded and led by Sam Walton (Walmart had 18 stores in 1969; today the store count is 4,742), and then Amazon by Jeff Bezos, it was virtually impossible for Sears/Kmart to survive—they did not!

These major retailers, together with others, including Meijer (formally Meijer Thrifty Acres), Grand Rapids, Michigan; and Fred Meyer, Portland, Oregon, all remain significant retailers still today! Every one of the retail chains described offered decor products, including paint.

We were not without competition going after chain discount and home-improvement retail chains. Other manufacturers also saw the same market growth opportunities. One was United Coatings with high volume plants in Chicago, Memphis, and Los Angeles.

The company was owned and managed by two brothers, Jules and Fred Knapp. They were great people and astounding salesmen! Both our companies were selling, or attempting to sell, many of the same retail chains. Their two key customers were Walmart and Kmart; in most cases, they marketed private-label paint using the retailer's brand name.

We became friends with our paths crossing frequently. During one such occasion, Jules invited me to meet with him at their Chicago plant headquarters. I did so on July 22, 1974. I sat in Jules's huge office, where he asked me to leave Glidden and join his company.

"I have no idea how much you make," he said, adding, "whatever it is, I will double."

In his office, I noticed a red light flashing in the ceiling corner. "What is that for?" I inquired.

He replied, "The light is connected to the filling line in the plant. If it stops flashing, it tells me that there is a production jam or filling interruption. It signals me to get involved and rectify the problem!" I had never considered leaving Glidden, and this was not the time!

Living and working in Cleveland was a new experience! The Glidden headquarters was located on the ninth floor of the Union Commerce Building (downtown), on the corner of Euclid and East Ninth Street (now called the Huntington Building).

The team I was working with were incredible people, all of whom were under the management and direction of Gary Bechtel and John Dumble (who both reported to Bill Kinsell, our president). Each one listed below was responsible for the nationwide support of their designated areas.

They were as follows: Mel Gilmer, company-owned store operations; Ed Kane, market research manager; Bob Lechner (succeeded by Charlie Carpenter), director of Advertising; Jerry Amato, retail marketing manager; Jack Brennan, national credit manager; Jim Shultz, related products manager; Fred Senko, manager, traditional dealer sales; Jim Russell (succeeded by John Ellis), painter maintenance; and me, national accounts manager.

This headquarters team managed and supported our regional trade sales managers (in the field) who were our direct connection to the field sales organization and company-owned and managed stores, which numbered, at the time, some 225 district centers and a separately managed chain of some 120 retail paint stores.

They were Mike Tweardy, Central; Don Liesen, Midwest; Eddie Bender, Southwest; Julian Clark, West; Don Reilly, Southeast; Alan Aungst, East; Bev Pugh, Canada. Within each region was a painter maintenance sales manager and a dealer sales manager. District centers (contractor stores ranging in size from 3,000 to 10,000 sq. ft.) were in most cities throughout the country; they serviced the coatings needs of paint contractors and maintenance customers. In addition, the larger DCs serviced the needs of our independent Glidden paint dealers.

This was an awesome team of people, highly motivated and very capable. We worked together seamlessly and effectively supporting the sales regions and customers.

Every year, national sales meetings would be held in each region, and we would all attend and deliver presentations covering new products, updated sales and marketing initiatives, and present awards to the top performers.

This occupied about six weeks of the late summer, traveling, in many cases, to resort locations within each region. There existed great camaraderie throughout our group, and we all enjoyed the experience of leading the sales teams to higher levels of accomplishment.

Each year, we would hire a celebrity or entertainer to join our group and participate in cocktail-hour presentations, and often they would perform in front of the entire regional sales organization.

Don Allen, a talented magician, was my favorite, and he inspired me to learn magic tricks and create a routine of my own! He performed a live magic show at all seven regional meetings one year and was a great hit.

I was living on the west side of Cleveland, in a condo attached to a nice residential neighborhood called King James. I had been dating a girl whose roommate was getting married, and I was invited to the wedding.

My girlfriend was out of town on the wedding day, and my mother happened to be visiting me from Atlanta, so she joined me. It was an outdoor wedding and a magnificent day. As the bridal party gathered for the ceremony, I spotted a beautiful young woman among them. Turning to my mother, I said, "See that girl in the polka-dot dress, I am going to marry her!"

My mother smiled politely and made no comment; she was used to her never-married thirty-four-year-old bachelor son making wild predictions! Well, this time, it was not so wild. I met Susan at the wedding reception afterward; our first date was the following evening, and on our next get-together, I asked her to marry me!

Turns out, she was the sister of the groom, Mike Bell, at whose wedding we met! December 21, 1973, was our wedding day, just four months later! As of this writing, we have been happily married for fifty years, have two daughters, two great sons-in-law, and seven incredible grandchildren.

Plus, I must add that the parents of both our sons-in-law are terrific people, whom we have become great friends with, Chuck and Sue Cox and Ronnie and Chris Harrell. Who says love at first sight is not real?

The new account dealer business grew with our taking advantage of the DIY and discount chains expansions. We also had a secret weapon in the name of Charlie Carpenter. Charlie was our advertising director guru, and he knew the business well; however, he had another asset—he was the best salesman I have ever met!

He developed a sales presentation format that we called the Big Boards. It was simple, and it really worked. Ahead of our sales presentation, Charlie and I would develop a sales dollar budget for the total store chain and annualize it, then we would allocate an ad allowance normally in the region of 5 percent of projected net sales. So if we calculated that the total store chain would purchase, say, $4 million in a year, we would establish an advertising budget of $200,000.

Charlie would then get the print rates (and TV costs if appropriate) in their markets. He would have presentation boards made (measuring 4'×6') incorporating aggressive print ads, one board for every month of the year. They were great ads with huge visual impact using massive price points. We made sure that the budget—say, in this example, $200,000—covered 100 percent of the ad costs.

We would then make sure that at our presentation, we had, in addition to buyers, the top management; most often I would separately communicate with the chief merchant and/or the president/CEO and convince them to be in attendance.

"This will be like no vendor presentation you have ever seen," I told them.

Charlie always made the ad presentation; he was a master, and the audiences always listened carefully because after all, he was *not* a *salesman*, he was an *advertising* guy—they trusted him! He would present each board separately, one at a time, explaining in great detail the power of the print message, along with the budgeted retail sales we forecasted that would be generated.

At the end of the presentation, the final Big Board would have on it—in *huge* type—the total dollar value of our financial commitment, say $200,000. Charlie's final words often were, "Ladies and gentlemen, this is our *commitment* to your business and to our *new partnership*." It was an incredible sales presentation format, and it blew the audience away every time!

Indeed, this presentation format, developed by Charlie, was so successful in securing new business that we began using it when presenting annual reviews with existing major customers. The concept was the same: we calculated the annual dollars that their forecasted sales would generate and then tailored an ad campaign to match, with Glidden paying for it. In reality, the money was generated by the sales into which we had built the ad allowance.

We often flew first class to our meetings. It worked like this: Many presentations we made were in the Northwest US (Ernst, Pay'n Pak, and Fred Meyer). Glidden only allowed coach! We routinely would use red-eye flights from Cleveland to Portland and Seattle, and on one of our early flights, boarding in Cleveland at about 11:30 p.m., the crew seemed half-asleep, and most of the first-class seats were empty; so we just sat there—no one took any notice. We had a nice meal and several free cocktails.

From that point on, this became our flight routine to the Northwest and other cities. Not once were we ever apprehended and moved to the back of the plane. We were like a couple of kids cheating at school!

Fred Senko, who was now heading up the independent dealer sales program, determined that we should create a mini version of Charlie's Big Board presentation and make it available to all the dealer sales reps nationwide.

With Charlie's help and input, he developed this format called the Red Box Presentation. Basically it consisted of a red foldout presentation box with preprinted presentation boards. They could be customized to incorporate the financials as necessary. It was a big hit with the dealer sales reps and helped to further expand this important business segment.

In summary, thanks to the sales strategy that Charlie created and implemented, presenting the most effective means of product sell through, Glidden's dealer sales grew dramatically in the years ahead!

One day, I was sitting in Charlie's large corner office when Bill Kinsell, CEO and our boss, walked in and then closed the door—made us a little nervous!

"Gentlemen, our sales of Spred Satin"—this was our lead product which we relied on for growth, prosperity, and maintaining our market leading role—"have leveled off, and I fear are headed for decline unless we take some immediate corrective action." We blinked. He continued, "I want you both to come up with a plan specifically designed to sell one million gallons of Spred Satin next month. Let's meet tomorrow in my office at 2:00 p.m. to review your ideas." He left abruptly!

Charlie and I looked at each other; a million gallons were a ton of product. He grinned and said, "There is only one way we can do this."

Charlie got an artist's pad in front of him, and he was drawing a frame of a full newspaper page. Inside it he drew a huge can of Spred Satin, and then above this and to the right, he drew a huge price, the same size as the paint can—$6.99. At the very bottom of the ad, he added two words: *Factory Sale*.

"You are kidding!" I said! "Our dealer customers have a cost of about $7 a gallon right now, and the market retail across the USA is in the $14 range."

"Precisely," Charlie replies. "If he wants to sell a million gallons, this is the only way it will work."

I agreed. Charlie picked up the phone and called Bob Iredell, the lead VP at Meldrum & Fewsmith, our advertising agency. The task was simple to describe—we needed the ad created and impactful by 10:00 a.m. tomorrow.

The ad was not just eye-catching—it took your breath away! At 2:00 p.m., we were in Bill's office; the ad was covered up.

"Well," he said.

Charlie replied, "Here is your million-gallon factory-sale ad."

He opened it up and displayed the ad. Silence. He then added, "The print ads will need to be run nationally and a specially produced TV commercial must run in all our major markets. We need your okay to proceed today."

Bill then inquired about the dealer's cost ramifications, and I explained that we would sell in and replenish product at the conclusion of the sale, contributing an amount of free Spred Satin that will recover a portion of the retailers' profit margin. I produced a page with all the numbers supporting this.

"Let's do it," he said. "Confirm the timing, communicate with our sales regions and with the dealer network nationally."

The sale ran; it did work, and over a million gallons were sold. This also generated a continuing momentum for our Spred Satin sales and certainly helped the long-term health of the product. It was a costly exercise for Glidden and many of our customers; particularly the big chains were not fully onboard with the pricing concept or the mechanics. One other by-product of this event was that we established a long-standing promotional umbrella—*'Factory Sale'*—which we used many more times in the future.

Managing major retail chains was not without its challenges. The Daylin Corporation, mentioned earlier, was run by Sandy Sigiloff in the western states. I was handling all their chains: Gulf Mart Miller, Handy Dan, and Angels.

One day our credit manager, Jack Brennan, came into my office and told me that Daylin was on the brink of bankruptcy and that we had to cut them off. Problem was that Handy Dan, by far their best division, was a significant Glidden account and were not, at the time, a part of the filing.

They were being run by Bernie Marcus and Arthur Blank, two of the best merchants I had ever met.

"No way," I retorted. "They are one of the very best customers we have. If you want to cut them off, we first have to meet with these guys." This was a smart ploy. I knew that once I got Jack in front of Bernie Marcus, there would be a favorable resolution.

I set up a meeting, and we flew out to California and met with Bernie and Arthur. They were great merchants and negotiators. By the time our lunch meeting was over, Jack had extended their line of credit and was totally satisfied that Handy Dan was a surviving component of Daylin. Little did we know at the time that these two guys would later revolutionize the DIY market in North America!

11

Toronto, Canada: Glidden Headquarters

My next assignment came along on January 21, 1977, when I was transferred to Toronto as general manager for the Canada region.

There had been a huge financial deficit at the prior year end, and the controller and general manager had been removed as a result. So along with Earl Kieffer (a senior CPA/accountant from Glidden's western region), I was brought in to clean up the mess and build back the business, reinstating a sound financial and marketing organization.

Meanwhile back in Cleveland, I hired Wayne Kilbey to replace me to handle the dealer and national account business. He was a Canadian running a Glidden district center in Thunder Bay, Ontario, a terrific salesman and perfect for his new job. More on Wayne later!

Sue and I had had our first child, Heather, in Cleveland, and she was not too wild about the move. Particularly when on a house-hunting trip in Toronto, the cab driver said to me, "Welcome to Canada. We love the Brits but are not too keen on the Americans coming into our country." He assumed Sue was a Brit! Not a good welcome!

One of the big challenges that Earl and I confronted when we arrived in Toronto, we were reporting to the top management in Cleveland, yet in Toronto there remained two executives: Jim Fowler (CEO) and Don Smythe, who were positioned as the regional director. They were both slated for retirement but were not yet out of the door, so to speak!

While they welcomed both of us to the team, we were significant outsiders, and even as figureheads, they retained considerable power and certainly had the respect and support of the entire Canadian operation. Essentially Earl and I were seen as outsiders brought in to turn around the ship. Happily they were two great people and supported us both in the job at hand.

We soon settled in, and I enjoyed the great friendship of Bev Pugh, who, a few years earlier, was the Glidden trade sales manager and had left to start his own business. We had our second daughter, Holly, and settled into the Canadian culture and lifestyle. Bev was her godfather.

There were significant changes that had to be made to the structure of the sales force and the financial components that Earl managed. My initial action was to meet with all our key accounts. Challenge was that Canada is about 22 miles wide, and the extreme length of the country is 5,780 miles. So business travel was long. A major customer, Federated Co-Op, was located in Saskatoon, Saskatchewan, which is 1,728 miles from Toronto! Alaska was also a part of my responsibility. Thus I traveled constantly, even to Alaska, where we had a paint distributor.

Toronto was a great city, and of course, we got caught up in the hockey world. Jerry Butler, who played for the Toronto Maple Leafs, was a neighbor and friend, so we became fans.

We lived in a western suburb called Mississauga that became famous one evening, on November 10, 1979, when a train hauling propane tanks through the city, derailed. The entire city, including ourselves, were evacuated and moved into downtown hotels for a week while the contamination and danger was removed.

One morning, my secretary, Pauline McManus, came in my office to announce that a Bernie Marcus from Home Depot was on the phone.

"Great," I said.

"Not great," she replied. "He sounds very upset!"

She was correct. Bernie Marcus, the Home Depot cofounder, had recently moved his team, along with his partner, Arthur Blank, and top merchant, Pat Farrah, to Atlanta. Atlanta was the first market they planned to launch Home Depot stores; two were planned for June 22, 1979. I picked up the phone, and Bernie led the conversation.

"I am sitting here in Atlanta, planning to open my first two stores in a few short weeks, and your people at Glidden are refusing to sell your paints to me! I need your immediate help!"

I was stunned. How in the world could any sane manufacturer turn down Home Depot as a customer! "Bernie, this has to be a crazy mistake," I responded. "Who are you talking to?"

"The top people," he replied.

"Let me make a phone call, and I will be right back with you," I said.

I immediately phoned my boss in Cleveland, CEO Bill Kinsell. He went to great pains to explain that Atlanta and the surrounding southeast markets were dominated with many, many progressive *independent* Glidden paint dealers, many of which—he reminded me—that I had sold when I was a territory rep there! He went on to reiterate that the total sales volume of the independent dealers in the area was very significant and would be lost if Home Depot were to sell our paints!

He added that a major customer, Glidden Gastonia, a million-dollar-plus account, would be surely lost. I failed in my quest; they were not going to sell Home Depot. I phoned Bernie back; difficult conversation—he was not happy, nor was I. Most folks in the US retail marketplace knew that this new big-box chain was going to totally dominate DIY. Dupont Lucite was the lead paint supplier when Home Depot opened their first Atlanta stores, and Glidden's Spred Satin was absent.

Having delivered the bad news to Bernie, I said to him, "What are your next markets?"

"Hollywood and Ft. Lauderdale in Florida," he said.

Big sigh of relief. Glidden's penetration on these markets was minimal. He cautioned me not to assume he would ever carry Glidden paints in these or any other stores!

When the time came for these southern Florida markets to open, Home Depot did carry our products, and the sales volume they generated was monumental and totally off the wall! Our paints were quickly added to all the Atlanta stores, and again, the sales volumes generated were beyond amazing! Today Glidden remains a major paint supplier delivering to Home Depot, huge dollars in annual sales!

12

Solid Paint

When originally moving to Canada from Glidden's Cleveland head-quarters, I had great support and communication with my former US colleagues, and they were all interested in my escapades and to find out how our Canada business differed from the USA.

Ed Kane, the US market research manager, approached me ahead of my move with the following story: Seems that several years ago, the Glidden Canada lab in Toronto had developed a unique and innovative product called solid paint. This product, I was told, revolutionized the paint industry in that one could apply paint without an applicator—no brush or roller required. Instead, one could simply stroke the surface to be painted with a solid cube of paint, similar, say, to taking a stick of butter and stroking it onto a horizontal or vertical surface.

Ed told me that no one in the US had ever seen the product, except our CEO, Bill Kinsell (who authorized its development), and that it was very top secret. My good friend Ed was counting on my sharing details of this product now that I was working in Canada!

Therefore, shortly after my arrival in Toronto, I visited our lab and asked to see our solid paint product and have a demonstration. I won't describe it right now. I called Ed in Cleveland, and we set a date for him to visit us in Toronto. I then booked his hotel room at the Airport Sheraton. I instructed the front desk to give him a room with an adjoining door to the next room.

Ed arrived, checked in at the hotel, and we went to his room. I then opened his side of the adjoining door and gave him a package of solid paint, saying, "Okay, Ed, here is the product, go paint the door!"

To expose the paint, one had to strip away a serrated cardboard area, expose the solid paint, and then apply. I could tell by the expression on his face that this was not going to be a *wow* experience. It was not; the product did not perform. The door was a ghastly mess smeared unevenly with paint, and looked awful. We closed the door, and for all I know, the unsightly paint application is still present to this day!

Truth is neither Ed nor I were surprised; any product kept under such cloak and dagger surveillance for so long had to be questionable! Despite the product becoming dead on arrival, so to speak, it did have some future value. While it was not capable of being applied to large surfaces, we did learn to apply it quite well to small flat boards that had no trim to cut in to.

We began to showcase the product in Canada, principally presenting and demonstrating it on small primed boards, and heralding it as a revolutionary new product for the "future." Remarkably there was significant interest and praise for our innovation in an industry that lacked new product creativity! We decided to present it to many of our key US customers and prospects, and they, too, were impressed.

This continued for about a year during which time we hoped that further technical refinement would improve the product, rendering it commercially viable. Unfortunately this never happened.

After three years running the trade sales business in Canada, I received a phone call from my boss, Bill Kinsell, in March 1981, asking me to come to Cleveland for lunch the following week to discuss a senior management position he wanted me to take on back at the Cleveland headquarters.

That evening, I announced to my wife that we might have to move to Cleveland. One would imagine this would be well received because she was not too keen on living in Canada, and Cleveland was her hometown, where her parents were still living. "I don't necessarily want to move back to Cleveland," she retorted! (I agreed with her).

So with this as background, I met with Bill Kinsell and Jack Muller for lunch in Cleveland, and before they brought up the subject, I resigned. Plain and simple, nothing personal. I explained, "We have two young girls, and we just don't want to live and bring them up in a northern US city." I explained that Atlanta would become our new home.

They were great and asked me to stay in Canada for four months, hire and train my replacement, and in return, they would cover all our costs associated with selling our Toronto home and moving to Atlanta, plus a generous severance agreement. It was a very amicable plan, and I will always have great respect and gratitude for both these leaders of our company.

Back in Canada, it was an easy job selecting my replacement— Steve Kluskowski, a French Canadian running the Glidden Ottawa operation; he was a strong manager and a perfect replacement.

Sue, the children, and I remained in Toronto for four months. Transitioning back to the USA, we finally made the move on July 4, 1981, direct to Atlanta.

My plan, when originally deciding to move back South, was to set up and establish a manufacturer's rep agency, selling decorative products. The advantage I had was that during the four months' transition in Canada, there was no secret about my plans, and I was therefore able to freely meet with manufacturers as I sought product lines to represent.

13

Atlanta, Georgia: Horsley Marketing Services Inc.

We arrived in Atlanta July 4, 1981, and rented a home in Dunwoody as our base of operations. Bernie Marcus was my first business contact. He took me to lunch; it was exciting to hear details of his Home Depot store progress and, of course, their recent NASDAQ listing. I set up and registered my business as Horsley Marketing Services, HMS, Inc. I was off and running! I really had no track record or manufacturer relationships that would help me secure product lines to represent, so I worked the phones for days on end.

My big break came in September 1981. A very good friend from the UK, Stewart Glanfield, called me and announced that he and his wife were traveling from their home in London to Hilton Head on vacation. Would Sue and I join them? We did!

Stewart, together with his business partner, Mervyn Fogel, ran a national chain of wallpaper and paint stores in the UK called Home Charm. The Fogel family owned the Home Charm chain of wallpaper and paint stores in the '70s. Mervyn Fogel, the scion of the family created a new chain of homecare superstores called Texas Homecare. Stewart joined the group from Valspar Paints and became joint managing director.

During the '60s, a major UK DIY chain named B&Q was launched and became a very successful big-box retailer. Before I immigrated to the US, I had sold ICI Dulux paints to these store groups. B&Q today are the leading home-improvement retailer in the UK.

Stewart and his wife, Maureen, are party people, and the Hilton Head trip was a blowout! He had great interest in the US decorative market and wanted to help me establish my rep business. His real passion was wallpaper, not paint! He knew more about the wallcoverings industry than anyone else in the business.

At the time, he said that there were two very significant North American drivers in wallcoverings: Norwall, a modern and successful wallpaper manufacturer in Toronto; and Brewster, a major wallpaper distributor located in Boston. They were owned respectively by Derek Ashton and Ken Grandberg.

Stewart set up meetings for me. I visited and met with both in 1981 (Brewster on November 15, and Norwall on November 17) and elected to work directly with Norwall. Reason being, they were a manufacturer (with a very modern state-of-the-art equipment). Brewster was a top-ranked distributor who focused their business on selling from wallpaper-pattern books.

14

Brampton, Ontario:
Norwall Wallcoverings

Norwall at the time was only interested in selling to DIY chains who would *stock* their wallcoverings. Derek quickly taught me that selling from wallpaper books was an expensive route to market, due largely to the high cost of producing wallpaper pattern books.

I became Norwall's sales agent throughout the USA, working with support from Derek Ashton and his Canadian sales manager, Doug Lambert, who also directly handled two US customers, Kmart and Pay'N Pak. At the time, they were the only two major Norwall accounts in the USA.

Doug was a great salesman, his customers loved him, and he provided me with valuable guidance and support. No question that wallpaper was a very different product from paint and, in many decor aspects, a step ahead! Wallpaper's decor attributes were quite unique—multicolor, textured, designer—a product that really changes the character of a room.

Norwall also produced a unique wallcovering called Expanded Vinyl. This wallpaper is manufactured using special-colored inks that, when heated, will expand and create a raised and textured design. Rotary screens are used in the manufacturing process, and as the wallcovering is printed, it passes through an oven which heats the inks, causing their expansion. The product is also called Textured Vinyl.

This same expanded process can also be used to print white textured wallpaper designs, with no colored printing inks used. Ideal if one wants a textured wall design with a soft white color as opposed to a colored design. One can install this white wallpaper and then apply a coat of paint—the color of one's choice! Hence the name Paintable Textures. This product was originally developed and marketed in the UK and remains most popular to this day. Graham & Brown, a major UK wallcoverings manufacturer, was and still is a leading producer. Much more about this company later!

Historically wallpapering has endured some negatives due largely to the fact that it is not as easy to install as paint. Furthermore, when it comes time for redecoration, removing it could be a challenge; whereas with repainting, you just applied one or two coats over the existing product!

In addition, wallpaper is typically more expensive to buy on a square-foot basis. Despite these factors, wallpaper popularity, though cyclical, continues to be widely used for interior decoration.

Back in the '80s, there was real interest and demand in the marketplace for wallpaper, and we were ready to write orders. The market was somewhat segmented; a retailer could purchase wallpaper books from a distributor, loan the books to their customer, they would select their pattern/design, calculate the number of rolls required, and place an order.

The cost of making pattern books was significant, and it was calculated at the time that the average wallpaper book placement in a retail store yielded less than fourteen rolls sold per annum! This was not the way Norwall operated! Their interest and sales strategy was confined to selling the product from a retail in-stock position.

With these criteria at hand, I went to work. The first account I sold in February 1982, was a small home center store chain headquartered in Savannah, called Builderama. Marvin Mednick was the buyer; his boss was Jim Smith, a merchant I knew from Forest City in Cleveland. It was a small but coveted first customer! A good beginning!

First, I had to establish the design assortment, the number of SKUs (stock keeping units or designs), inventory investment per store, and finally the space in which we had to supply fixtures to display the wallpaper. They were a twelve-store chain at the time and ideal for us to fine-tune the mechanics of setting up a new account.

That same year, July 11, 1982, I contacted Joe Craig, the Walmart paint buyer. At the time, they had 491 stores in the US, which included a large and growing number of giant "supercenter stores." My approach was to sell in-stock wallpaper to the supercenters. Joe insisted that he have *two* wallpaper suppliers, so I suggested a fifty-fifty Norwall/Imperial split (Imperial was a competing and highly successful wallpaper manufacturer). He agreed to this plan, and in concert with Dan Collins, Imperial's national sales manager, we teamed up and set and merchandised the stores as a team on May 16, 17, 18, and week of June 13.

The next account I secured was Sherwin-Williams. Wayne Kilbey, who had taken over my Cleveland dealer sales job, left Glidden and joined Sherwin-Williams. Their headquarters office was also in Cleveland, about half a mile from Glidden.

He had a big job and managed the stores' division comprising over two thousand retail and wholesale paint stores throughout the US. We were good friends, and he invited me to fly up to Cleveland and meet with him on January 3, 1983, with the promise that he would introduce me to his wallpaper buyer, Bill Sweeney.

We had a great meeting, and I presented the idea of placing in every Sherwin-Williams store a cardboard constructed wallpaper display tower that would merchandise twenty-four different patterns. Bill bought into the concept, selected the twenty-four designs, and the order totaled just over a million dollars.

The sale event was so successful that the following spring, he repeated the promotion, with two towers per store for yes—two million dollars. John Keenan, the Norwall comptroller, called me in Atlanta when he was about to mail this commission check to me; he was choking!

As the Norwall business was growing, I needed additional sales professionals to keep the momentum going. With a free hand on hiring, I began to recruit some of my old friends who were still with Glidden.

Jim Sarlie, Peter Hill, Bob Wissink, and Jim Neal joined HMS. Irv Hurd was the first hire; he was not with Glidden but had huge experience and capability in the selling field. These guys were real heavyweights, and they just loved the opportunity to escape the corporate world and enjoy the freedom and excitement of an entrepreneurial sales environment.

They were amazing to work with; we were all making good money, and our boss, Derek Ashton, was happy as a clam! Plus, we all became great friends and an awesome team.

We also had a secret weapon! Derek loved airplanes! First, he had a King Air, and later he upgraded to a Westwind. The planes were totally at our disposal; they hangared in Toronto but, at a moment's notice, would fly to, say, Atlanta, pick me up or one of our team, go and pick up a customer or prospective customer, fly to Toronto, tour the factory (which was a showpiece in itself), and meet with Derek to discuss a business partnership. I cannot begin to describe how much business this accommodation produced for us.

I had a meeting with a Sears buyer in Chicago, who was in the decor area, Joe McGroarty, on January 23, 1987.

"Joe," I said, "if you really want to consider wallpaper, in stock for your customers, then you need to come to our factory in Toronto. I will pick you up at Meigs Field Airport, go meet with Derek, the owner, see specifically how we can support Sears stores, and we will have you home in time for dinner."

He made the trip. His boss, Bill Straus, joined us, and by the time we landed in Toronto and then back in Chicago, we were all best friends. What a way to conduct business!

This new Sears account was an awesome success. They decided to use two wallpaper suppliers, one for the western half of the country and another for the eastern half.

"Which half do you want?" Joe asked!

"The east," I responded. We got it! Our competitor, Imperial Wallcoverings, got the western half of the country. There is way more wallpaper sold in the east!

Sears, at the time, was managed by regional VPs, and these were the people we had to work with as we set up the new in-stock program. They were a great team of people and very committed to our new business.

Fred Clackler was the southeast guy, located in Atlanta, a terrific manager who was a total Roll Tide enthusiast. Little did I know that my eldest daughter would one day go to Alabama! All the wallcoverings display racks were manufactured by Abrams Fixture in Atlanta, engineered by their manager, Jim McNabb, who also coordinated their shipment to stores concurrent with the initial shipment of wallpaper orders. Our team set up the program in each store, and the Imperial program was merchandised alongside by their sales manager, Dan Collins.

As the Norwall business continued to grow, Derek started to look for new business partnerships, one was with Lennon Wallpaper in Joliet, Illinois. He befriended the owner, Walter Mueller, and began to talk about merging the two companies.

However, Lennon was an old-line manufacturer and was totally focused on the wallpaper-pattern book—special-order business. The very market that Derek had historically shunned and ignored—with good cause!

They eventually merged the two companies, and the result was significant financial damage to Norwall. The banks got nervous and insisted that Derek hire an individual who could clean up and manage the merger. Bill Wilson was the man they hired on September 7, 1988, not a good choice! His first action was to examine the financials, and when he saw the income that I and the rest of my team was making, he was mortified!

About three months into his tenure, I received a phone call from Peter Hill, one of my sales guys, who said to me, "Tony, I just had lunch with Bill Wilson, and he offered me your job!"

"Oh really?" I said. "Did you accept?"

Am not sure he answered my question, but I parted company with Norwall on March 30, 1990.

I consulted with Derek, Norwall's owner; he had no part in this event, and he fired Bill Wilson the following month. Unfortunately the entire Lennon exercise was very damaging to Norwall's long-term prospects. As the Norwall sales director from 1982 to 1990, I spearheaded their US sales growth from $0 to $25 million annually.

15

Cape Breton Island, Nova Scotia: Cape Breton Wallcoverings

I was now in Atlanta, out of work! Just a week went by, and I received a phone call from a John Hooker. He is a Canadian friend from the past, and he said, "I want you to come and work for me." (Wonderful words!)

John used to work in Toronto for a mall-based wallpaper store chain called St. Clair Paint & Wallpaper. Seems that the owner, Louis Litwin, had recently purchased a wallpaper factory located in Cape Breton Island, called Cape Breton Wallcoverings. John was subsequently relocated to Cape Breton to manage the business.

John invited me to visit his factory; it is a two-plane trip: Atlanta to Halifax to Sydney. I arrived in this beautiful Nova Scotia island—hard to believe there was any commerce there! The factory was quite new and partly funded by the Canadian government. The wallcoverings they were producing are excellent quality, and they had modern screen machines that will print expanded vinyl. The very same product that Norwall and Graham & Brown—mentioned earlier—were producing.

The textured and paintable aspects were identical. Furthermore, it's texture, combined with the thickness of the product, served to cover up and hide wall imperfections and irregularities. Indeed, it would also cover paneling grooves, a unique feature particularly for those homeowners who wanted to be rid of paneled walls that had once, in the past, been a favored and widely used wall substrate, particularly in rec rooms and basements.

The plant tour was impressive; we agreed on a commission rate, and John indicated that he had a rep on the West Coast that I may want to partner with; his name was Mike Reilly. This is important as I had excellent relations with the West Coast Home Depot buyers (Ron Carnes and Kathy Schagg), and it would be valuable to have someone to work locally with this buying office. Mike and I met, and shortly thereafter, we became partners.

We had a meeting with West Coast Home Depot. They loved our new product; we were back in business. Ron liked the expanded vinyl Cape Breton produced and quickly began executing promotional buys from us in full truckloads.

This product flew out of the stores; everyone was happy! Six months into this new business partnership, I asked Ron if there was a chance we could become a core wallpaper supplier rather than just selling him promotions. He was okay with this and set up a meeting with his boss, the Home Depot regional merchandise manager, Bill Hamlin, at an upcoming national home center show in Chicago, at the adjacent McCormick Inn Hotel.

We presented to Ron and his boss, Bill, a terrific range of products, principally expanded vinyl. They loved the product and particularly our idea to source the designs exclusively to Home Depot.

Bill Hamlin said, "We will commit to this program exactly as you have presented. Set it up and we will make the purchase, and it will be a part of our ongoing core program in all western stores."

We estimated that the value of this one initial order was in the region of $750,000 and annualized $4+ million.

It is important to mention that one aspect of conducting business with Home Depot that is unique and most valuable is as follows: When the buyer/merchant makes a verbal commitment, they stick to it; no ifs and buts. If they say, "Okay, let's go with this program, I will put it in my stores" (as did Bill Hamlin in this case), with such a statement, you could take it to the bank! Never once did I experience one of their buyers reneging on such a commitment! Some manufacturers would ask me, "Do you have a purchase order?" If I said no, they would get nervous.

I told them, "These guys are good for their word, trust me. Get the products ready to ship, the PO will be in the works!" It always was.

Our meeting with Ron and his boss was awesome, positive in every respect. Mike and I left on a cloud and proceeded to the nearest phone to communicate this great news to John Hooker at Cape Breton.

The phone rang and rang, eventually answered.

"John Hooker, please."

The response was, "We are the Financial Receivers of Cape Briton Wallcoverings. We have been appointed as custodian of their property and business operations necessary to secure their assets and affairs in order to pay their liabilities and debts. As of this time, they are essentially out of business."

This was a disaster, the end of the road for us! We quickly regrouped with our West Coast rep, Lou Knappenberger, and explained that Cape Breton was bankrupt! He seemed less concerned and told us he was confident that we would secure an alternative source! (More on our rep network shortly.)

This was not good; we had just consummated a significant business opportunity with Home Depot West Coast, and with one swipe, our product source was gone!

We returned to the home center show and to the Tile Pak booth, operated by Mervyn Fogel, a good friend in the tile business who was originally from the UK and was a founding member of the British B&Q store chain. He listened to our disastrous story and immediately said, "Call David and Roger. They would be a terrific supplier."

16

Blackburn, England: Graham & Brown Wallcoverings

www.grahambrown.com or scan barcode below

David Brown and Roger Graham were the owners and joint managing directors of a large UK wallpaper manufacturer, located in Blackburn, Lancashire, registered as Graham & Brown Ltd. (I had met them a few years back at a trade show in London.) Mike and I returned to the phone booths at the lower level of the McCormick Inn and phoned G&B.

Both David and Roger were on the line, and fortunately they remembered meeting me previously. Also, it turned out that they had knowledge of our USA relationships with Home Depot. I regret that it is not possible to emulate their very distinct Lancashire accents in writing, so I must tell you that it was *very* strong and *very* distinct!

I got straight to the point; we had secured a wallpaper order of close to a million dollars, our source of supply was bankrupt, we needed a new partner. "When can you come to Blackburn to discuss in greater detail and work out a plan?" they asked.

My response was that (a) there were two of us, and (b) we needed the funds for us both to fly to and stay in the UK.

"No problem. We will handle all that," was their response.

So on June 17, 1991, Mike and I flew to Manchester and were picked up at the airport by John Wenlock, the G&B chauffeur.

It was noon by the time we had checked in to the hotel, The Northcote Manor.

"David and Roger will be here shortly for lunch, meet them in the bar."

We quickly learned that a couple of pints of beer at lunch was the norm. Mike, my business partner, did not drink alcohol, so at least one of us would remain clearheaded.

The key members of the management team beneath David and Roger were John Carter (operations manager and nephew of David), Andrew Graham (UK sales director and son of Roger), Ian Brown (environmental and logistics manager, son of David), George Root (finance/comptroller, nonfamily member), and Mark Radford, Advertising and Marketing Director (nonfamily member). Henry Brown (David's father) founded the company together with Harold Graham (Roger's father). Harold was deceased, and Henry suited up each day and came into the office (or mill, as it was called) for a couple of hours.

First, we had a tour of the mill (manufacturing facility); very impressive, modern with the capability of huge production runs which yielded great cost efficiencies. We then visited the design studio, where the artists created the patterns and wallpaper designs.

We met Roger Fleet, a talented artist and designer who played a significant role later in our USA business, interfacing with our customers, often creating custom designs and wallpaper colorways, tailored to individual and different markets in the United States.

Roger remained a close friend and indeed is responsible for the creation of this book! Unhappily during a phone conversation we had together on October 3, 2021 (from me in Atlanta, with Roger in Blackburn, UK), he sustained a massive heart attack and died.

It was a tragic event. I immediately e-mailed his son Christain, who lived nearby, and alerted him of my concern, telling him that his father had dropped the phone and abruptly ended our phone conversation. He shortly reported back that when he arrived at the house, Roger was sitting in his chair, with the phone close by on the floor. This book is a tribute to his memory and great friendship.

One of the products we saw on our tour was white embossed wallpaper, technically described as Expanded Vinyl, the same product I described earlier, when discussing its production at Norwall and Cape Breton. This sounded exciting. Both the whites and colored textures were marketed under the Graham & Brown brand name of Super Fresco.

Because Super Fresco was so thick and textured, as previously mentioned, it had the capability of concealing defective cracked walls and even paneling! So we focused on these features in our sales presentations, and overnight the product became a huge success! Compounding this was the fact that at the time, no other wallpaper manufacturer was producing and marketing such a product in the USA.

The top photo on page 84 shows Super Fresco wallpaper applied over primed paneling. The fact that this white textured wallpaper could be painted was a huge plus for Home Depot! It became the top-selling wallpaper category and remained so permanently!

Our meeting with David and Roger was very productive, and we were relieved and stimulated by the fact that they had no existing representation in the USA. Because we had no income, they agreed to prepay commissions from the start, which would be adjusted and balanced as our sales volume developed. By month four, we produced and met the funding support, and from that point on, our commissions grew commensurate with sales.

This partnership grew into a solid win-win relationship. Our first action was to fulfill the Home Depot West Coast orders that were originally planned for shipment by Cape Breton Wallcoverings. The product just flew off the shelves! This allowed us to reach out to the other Home Depot divisions.

17

Monmouth Junction, New Jersey: Graham & Brown, USA

First challenge was the need to address the matter of distribution. There was no way we could service several hundred Home Depot stores from the factory in England! Fortunately in the past, G&B had worked with a commercial wallpaper distributor in New Jersey, run by a very aggressive and customer-focused person in the name of David Lee.

David was delighted to join forces with us and become the distribution arm for G&B in the USA. He was operating a warehouse in Monmouth Junction, New Jersey, which was ideal for our needs. Within a few short weeks, he was set up electronically, and there was product en route from the factory.

Within three months, we were able to begin selling Graham & Brown Wallcoverings to all Home Depot divisions, either direct to their warehouses or direct to store.

The drivers of this business were Home Depot veterans Pat Farrah and Jim Inglis. Pat was one of the original founders, and Jim, as executive vice president of merchandising, had a keen eye and love for the decor category. There were also several other merchants: Kim Curtin, Barry Silverman, and Dennis Johnston, to name three who strongly endorsed the sale of wallpaper. They saw the category as supporting their paint business and also driving *female* customers into their stores. From day one, Home Depot coveted and sought female shoppers!

As the Graham & Brown business continued to grow, it became clear that our USA wallcoverings business had grown to the point that we needed a marketing and administrative manager at our Monmouth Junction distribution operation. David had his own business to run, a successful commercial wallcovering company called TexTan.

David Lee, the original and current owner of the facility, had done a great job managing and distributing our wallcoverings. In addition, he provided our key accounts with point-of-sale support materials that were valuable tools helping to provide product focus in the stores.

With our business growth, Graham & Brown management in the UK decided that it was time that they had direct ownership and control over their US business, and asked Mike and I to seek a strong and experienced manager to run their operation. David was not too happy with the prospect of our hiring someone new to take on this responsibility! We proceeded and interviewed several candidates.

I had heard of Bill Woods through mutual contacts in the wall-covering industry and set up a meeting with him at our New Jersey distribution center. Bill and I sat together in a small conference room, discussing the industry and the management needs supporting our business. There was a speaker phone sitting on the center of the table, and halfway through the interview, David's voice boomed out loud with a question for me about an order he had just received.

I quickly concluded that if I could hear David, he could also hear me conducting my interview with Bill! Not wishing to make a big deal, I got up from my chair, walked calmly to the telephone cable in the baseboard, and ripped it out. Sat back down and contin-ued the interview.

Bill Woods was our choice, a great guy who had spent time in the wallcoverings business, was well connected, and ideal to support our sales reps and the product distribution. Following this meeting, Bill flew to the UK to meet with Roger Graham and David Brown—the business owners—for a final interview. They totally endorsed my recommendation, and Bill joined the company in April 1995, as VP of operations.

Bill was a perfect candidate for our business; he had an excellent knowledge of the wallcoverings industry and quickly took command of our field logistics needs, plus the hiring and supporting our network of independent sales representatives. In addition, he was active in the field and worked with and supported our rep groups. From time to time, Bill and I would travel together meeting with customers, prospects, and attending grand openings.

On one occasion, we were asked by the Graham & Brown management in the UK to meet with a drywall manufacturer in Baltimore. Seems that they were using their brand name, Super Fresco, for an embossed paneling product they produced. The Graham & Brown textured wallpaper was also called Super Fresco, though it was not a registered trademark; so there was concern that we might be infringing on their mark.

We made an appointment and traveled to their facility in Baltimore. The product they were marketing was quite unique. They produced half-inch-thick conventional drywall sheets and then individually compressed them to create a three-dimensional judge's panel measuring 4'×8'. The panels could then be applied directly to wall studs or over existing Sheetrock. The product was branded Super Fresco. Our meeting objective was to secure their agreement to using the same brand for our wallcovering.

Upon arrival, we were led into a conference room in which eight Hasidic Jews were waiting to meet with us. They were all dressed in orthodox clothing, hats included. Frank Fellone, an Italian, their general manager was the sole Gentile in the group.

We got to see their Super Fresco paneling, discussed our wallpaper product, and asked if we might use their Super Fresco brand given that our product was totally different in composition and application. They agreed to a fair and reasonable licensing agreement that Graham & Brown happily paid.

Bill also had the wherewithal and ability to work closely and in harmony with David Lee, both in the business transition and long-term support partnership. To this day, we still reflect and laugh about the removal of the phone cord during the interview!

We worked together building our North American business, and Bill was most instrumental in our business growth, customer support, and product supply logistics—all of which were manufactured in the UK. He subsequently was appointed president of the US operation and had a full registered voting seat on the UK G&B board of directors. We remain close friends to this day.

At this point, we had recruited a few independent manufacturers reps around the country to help us with our sales efforts. Now with Bill on the team, we formalized our structure throughout the USA, joining forces with a network of strong and well-connected rep companies.

Both Pat Farrah and Jim Inglis supported and believed in the wallcovering category and fought hard to make it work. Their leadership demanded store participation, and it happened. No question, without the commitment and input from Pat and Jim, we would have never achieved the penetration and success of our wallcoverings program.

David and Roger would regularly visit the United States, meeting with Jim in Atlanta, and Pat in California. Each time there was incredible comradeship and business rapport. While Home Depot had other wallpaper vendors, Graham & Brown was favored and well respected, partly since they had no other USA customers outside of Home Depot! It was a wonderful business relationship, and our volume of business grew significantly each year.

There was also a great rapport and strong relationship between the Graham & Brown management team and our network of reps supporting the Home Depot wallcoverings program. G&B were not familiar with or accustomed to the use of independent reps, and they saw our network as highly cost-effective and efficient in providing the training and merchandising needs of our products and programs in all the Home Depot stores. Particularly as Mike and I (HR wallcoverings) were paying the reps out of the total commissions we earned from G&B.

On several occasions, Graham & Brown hosted our rep network at their factory in Blackburn, England. These were big extravaganzas—product training, factory tour, and great food and accommodations—amply supported with alcoholic beverages. On one occasion, wives were included, and on another, an overnight in London for a theater visit. The largest and most extravagant trip was to celebrate the Graham & Brown fiftieth-year anniversary, when on this occasion, a number of Home Depot merchants also attended. The rapport and friendship among our reps and the Graham & Brown family was wonderful, unique, and significant! No question, this magnified the business success we all created and enjoyed.

18

Manufacturers' Representatives

Creating and managing a North American sales and marketing organization is no easy task! As we began to sell wallcoverings to retail store chains, we had to factor in our product manufacturing source in the UK, the point of distribution in Monmouth Junction, New Jersey, and the two founding partners, Mike Reilly (San Jose, California) and myself, Tony Horsley (Atlanta, Georgia).

The cost to recruit, employ, and train a team of sales and service representatives was clearly prohibitive. The best and only solution was to partner with *existing* independent rep groups around the country.

Such organizations existed and were located throughout North America, selling products to retail chains. We researched these many business operations, established our territorial/geographical needs, and sought rep groups that were selling to and servicing the retailers we were targeting and planning to sell our wallcoverings to. We also had to be sure that they were not already representing a wallpaper manufacturer, as this would be a conflict.

Beginning in June 1995, we began seeking, interviewing, and hiring a national network of independent manufacturers' representatives. Initially our focus was in the geographic markets that we had established and sold our wallcoverings to.

This exercise turned out to be easier than we anticipated. At the time we had, as earlier mentioned, established the beginnings of a sales relationship with Home Depot. They were expanding their store network across the country, so we had the opportunity of part-nering with rep organizations who were focused on these huge stores that were opening up.

Listed below are the rep groups we partnered with along with their areas of responsibility:

Graham & Brown North American rep groups
Pacific Marketing (California): Lou Knappenberger, Ty Olson
Pro Marketing (Southeast): Harvey Hall, Jay Hall, Rick Hall
Pro Marketing (Southwest): Greg Hall
Pro Marketing (Florida): Billie Hall
Harvey Gerstman & Associates (Northeast): Harvey Gerstman, Dan Gerstman
Mudd Lyman & Associates (Midwest): De Mudd, Larry Lyman
Lumbard & Associates (Northwest): Steve Lumbard, Pete Balserini
Cody & Associates (Canada): Neal Cody

Every one of these independent rep companies, their man-agement, and sales team were top-drawer sales and service profes-sionals. Most all of them were also established and working with Home Depot, who were expanding their store network across North America. Without them, we would never have succeeded in building a thirty-million-dollar wallpaper business!

19

Trade Shows

Each year, the hardware and home-improvement industry in the United States sponsors major trade exhibitions, enabling manufacturers and distributors to promote and display their products and services. These trade shows, as they are called, are organized by the National Retail Hardware Association (NRHA).

They are valuable events taking place annually in the spring—originally held in New York City, then at Chicago's McCormick Place Convention Center, and more recently at the Las Vegas Convention Center. The venue changes most probably reflect both improvement in weather conditions and lower costs for exhibitors and attendees!

Glidden, along with all the national paint manufacturers, participated along with major hardware producers and distributors. Wallcovering and decor suppliers also exhibit together with hardware and tools, electrical, plumbing, ceramic tiles, lawn and garden, barbecue grills, storage products, and paint applicators. In total, over 150 product categories are featured.

Six hundred fifty-plus companies exhibit. NRHA do not publish the number of show attendees, my best estimate is that it is in the region of two hundred thousand. It is a significant and valuable show, well attended, with a strong contingent of retailer decision-makers present. In addition, the show also draws exhibitors and attendees from around the world, providing a substantial international presence and participation.

In my days working for Glidden, Norwall, and representing Graham & Brown, I never missed a show! It was hard work setting up a booth and participating in back-to-back meetings with existing customers and prospects. The huge benefits were that at this one location, you could interact and communicate with many existing customers and have the opportunity to sell to new retail chains.

There were other benefits also; we were able to see our competition's new products, packaging, and sales messages, plus at the same time, being able to make assessments of their marketing strengths, weaknesses, and capabilities.

Another major benefit was meeting with many of our key *existing* customers with whom we could reinforce our business relationship and perhaps sell them additional product lines!

We would set up meetings ahead of the show with our key accounts. At most all shows I attended, I had very productive meetings with Home Depot merchants; they always attended the hardware show en masse, and it was valuable to meet with them, often at a pre-established group meeting.

Bernie Marcus, Arthur Blank, Jim Inglis, and Pat Farrah were always in attendance, at trade shows, working with suppliers and supporting and leading the City of Hope Cancer Research Foundation.

Trade shows are hard work but necessary, productive, and create value to your business in the long term.

20

Pension Plan

In 1992, Mike and I determined that it was time for us to establish an investment/pension/savings plan. We both realized that our business model would not last forever, and that we should initiate a long-term financial plan.

At this point, Mike had recently purchased a second home in Lake Tahoe, and I in Hilton Head. My suggestion was that we allocate and direct a portion of our monthly income toward the purchase of additional rental homes in these two popular vacation destinations.

Mike was against this idea and proposed that we establish a defined benefit pension plan into which we would purchase and establish stock market securities that would grow and provide us both with an income when we retired.

We agreed on this more secure and reliable pension format and directed our accountant, Lisa Chen, in San Francisco to set up this for us. I learned that a defined benefit plan is an ideal retirement vehicle for the self-employed, allowing one to reduce income taxes while funding one's retirement. The contributions grow tax deferred, and another plus was that this vehicle enabled us to invest sums of money, thereby building a meaningful pension plan in a short time frame.

Once set up, we were able to purchase within the plan, stocks, and mutual funds of our choice. For me, this was a new experience; I had previously never invested in securities and had no real understanding or capability. Fortunately Mike was well experienced and took the lead in selecting strong funds and stocks of successful well-managed companies. Home Depot, Hewlett Packard, and Vanguard Wellington at the time were among our top performers.

We later added our wives to the plan, which further strengthened our future incomes. When our business partnership dissolved, it was an easy process to split these assets equally in two. Thanks to Mike and this stock market learning experience, I still maintain and manage our two portfolios, mine and my wife's. Most of the positions have remained unchanged and commensurate with the market, the value has grown and remains today our principal source of income.

21

The Home Depot

Throughout my business career, Home Depot has remained a focal and pre-eminent component and occupies a large portion of the narrative in this book. I consider myself to be very fortunate to have witnessed and participated in their growth and success and can attest to their many strengths and successes.

Each year, they host a vendor meeting during which Pat Farrah would recognize and announce a vendor of the year within each key product category. Graham & Brown obtained this award often and did so for five consecutive years, from 1995 to 1999, within department 75, the decor category. This was probably a vendor record!

On the fifth occasion, Pat concluded his presentation to us, adding, "These Graham & Brown guys don't need to show up next year. I will announce in their absence the advertising dollar commitment for the year ahead!" One of the primary activities at these meetings was for the key vendors to commit to their advertising support dollars for the upcoming calendar year!

Always eager to differentiate from competitors and charter new concepts, Home Depot determined that there was an unserved market in rural America. Their solution—a new format store under the banner *Crossroads* was created, designed to serve farmers and ranchers in rural markets.

The first to open was in Quincy, Illinois, on July 20, 1995. Denny Ryan, a senior VP from the Atlanta headquarters, headed up the project. Jim Shalda was the decor merchant, whom we knew well in his former role as their Midwest buying office. We featured an extensive wallpaper presentation; after all, farmhouses get decorated too!

This was a unique grand opening attended by many of the top Home Depot team. We invited David and Roger, the Graham & Brown owners, to attend. They flew into O'Hare from the UK, and with Quincy in the middle of rural Illinois, we chartered a plane to take the four of us to the event.

The grand opening was exciting, well attended, with speeches and much fanfare. The store was one of a kind, offering farm equipment, tools, clothing, decorating products, and yes, animal food! A total of five stores were opened before management determined that Home Depot Crossroads did not fit their image or brand; they were closed. Credit goes to them for thinking outside the big box.

The next grand opening I attended in 1995 was in San Juan, Puerto Rico, along with Bill Woods, our newly appointed operations manager. This was on July 23, just three days after the Crossroads opening. The event was quite different; the new Home Depot store was mobbed with people clamoring to buy merchandise. At one point, the fire department closed the entry doors to the store and removed several hundred shoppers, claiming the overcrowding represented a serious fire hazard.

These grand-opening events provided an opportunity for us to demonstrate products to the many customers, often visiting a Home Depot store for the first time. Our Super Fresco Paintable Textures were ideal, as the ability to cover damaged or paneled walls was quite unique. We also marketed paintable borders that were ideal for application around a ceiling line or at midchair-rail level.

At the Puerto Rico grand opening, we set up a large trestle table upon which, using a four-inch roller, applied bright-colored paint to the borders. The customers loved it and were fascinated by the ability to custom paint textured wallpaper. This exercise resulted in significant sales of these products.

We attended most all grand openings; it gave us valuable interactions with the customers, and we were able to meet and communicate with both store and corporate headquarters management. Over time, we established strong relationships with Home Depot employees at all levels, which, in the long term, served to strengthen our business partnership and success.

In 1996, Mike and I became greedy and came up with the idea of selling wallcoverings to another major retailer. We made a call to the Walmart buyer, Assam Ansari, got an appointment, traveled to Bentonville, Arkansas, presented a strong in-stock wallpaper program, and at the conclusion, Assam said, "I like your proposal. How do you want to proceed?"

Surprised at the speedy and positive response, I said, "Give us one hundred stores to test and demonstrate the strength of our program."

He said, "Done!"

We left and headed home, having phoned David and Roger with the news. They were exuberant; particularly as of late, they had become concerned with having so many eggs in one basket in the USA. Mike and I flew to our respective cities. That night, I lay in bed and said to myself, what in the world have I done? I am selling product to the largest and best home-improvement retail store chain in the world who supports our products 100 percent, and now I have offered one of their major competitors the opportunity to compete on equal terms! Am I crazy or what! No sleep that night!

The next day, I phoned David and Roger and expressed my concerns and reservations, plus Mike's, who was somewhat in agreement with me. They were not totally onboard with my thinking, and I suggested that at an upcoming home center show in Chicago some three weeks away, we meet with Jim Inglis to discuss. They said okay, and I agreed to set up a meeting.

Jim Inglis routinely held high level Home Depot key vendor meetings during the show in his suite. He agreed to slot in David and Roger. The day arrived, and it was determined that David would lead the topic and announce our intent to sell to another major national retail chain. Jim and his large team of senior merchants were in the suite. It was a formidable group, and I was very nervous; Jim was a strong and seasoned VP of merchandising, known for his lack of patience with vendors who either did not perform or did not please him!

David was the bad guy and handled the announcement that we were planning to sell wallcoverings to another national chain retailer. The room was silent. Everyone looked at Jim, who said, "Who might that be?" David answered the question; this time, a longer silence!

Jim cleared his throat and said, "David, I just do not believe that such a move will gain you any significant market share improvement. What can we do at Home Depot to better support your business to the point that you will not feel it is necessary to expand your retail distribution in the US? Perhaps you can document your response with specifics on how we can strengthen our business together and expand your wallpaper sales and market share growth throughout the Home Depot national network of stores."

The tension relaxed significantly in the room! We agreed to follow up as Jim had requested, and the meeting concluded with firmer-than-normal handshakes!

We regrouped after the meeting and determined that our long-term future and business growth in the USA was best tied to Home Depot. We drafted an agreement between Graham & Brown and the Home Depot, which essentially asked that they would purchase Paintable Textures exclusively from us and that their wallpaper program would represent an agreed-to percent of their total core assortment. They okayed the plan, and we moved forward with a strong and cooperative business relationship. Our partnership continued to flourish, and in the year 2000, our sales to them surpassed $30 million (see Appendix 3).

At this point, we were selling wallcoverings successfully to all Home Depot USA divisions, including a store they had opened in Santiago, Chile. A competing home center, Sodimac, was in the same city, and we decided to take a trip down to Chile to meet with them, as they had expressed an interest in wallcoverings with the owners of Graham & Brown. Together with Bill and Mike, we established a meeting date—March 23, 1999.

We flew into Santiago, checked into our hotel, and the following day, embarked on a two-hour taxi drive to the Sodimac buying office. Halfway there, we began planning our meeting strategy.

"Who has the samples?" I asked. Our goal was to sell them an in-stock program of our Super Fresco Paintable Textured wallcoverings, an ideal product for the construction of older homes and commercial buildings in Chile.

As previously discussed, Super Fresco Paintable Textures is ideal for application over uneven and even cracked walls and ceilings; plus it can be painted the color of the user's choice.

Sodimac was not selling such a product, so we decided this would be the focus our presentation. Again I asked from the back seat of the taxi, "Who has the samples?"

Silence.

Seems that in all our hurrying to get on the road trip to the buying office, none of us had packed any product sample rolls or small sections of paneling onto which we routinely applied the heavily textured wallcovering. This was a compelling component of our presentation—demonstrating how the product covered paneling grooves and irregularities!

As luck would have it, in the bottom of my briefcase, I had just one 3"×5" single fold leaflet describing the product and bearing two small photographs. That was it! We met with the buyer, and after the normal introductions and thanks-for-meeting-with-us conversations, we proceeded to describe the product. Halfway through the presentation, I ceremoniously produced the leaflet and used it (as best I could) to articulate the spectacular properties of the heavily textured wallcovering.

It was a cordial meeting, and there was strong interest by Sodimac to sell our paintables. It was also a lesson for all of us: Before traveling to make a customer or prospect presentation; create a checklist of all the supporting props and samples you will need and pack them ahead of time. In addition, when international trips are involved, ship a duplicate set of meeting samples to the buyer well ahead of your meeting!

We took the opportunity to visit the Home Depot store in Santiago, who was already selling our wallcoverings. Clearly both retailers were in direct competition and neither wanted us to sell our products to both parties. We happily complied and just remained a supplier to Home Depot.

A wonderful book authored by the founders, Bernie Marcus and Arthur Blank, with Bob Andelman, was published in 1999 and titled *Built from Scratch*. It is the story of the creation and incredible success of Home Depot and the many unique and marvelous initiatives they employed in the creation and management of the company. I would describe it as a unique business textbook that should be read by every retail and wholesale organization who aspires to serve their customers well and become successful! The cover proudly states, *How a Couple of Regular Guys Grew the Home Depot from Nothing to $30 Billion.*

As mentioned, our wallcoverings business with Home Depot reached a similar type of milestone in 2000, when we achieved sales to their stores of $30.5 million! At this time, Home Depot was maturing yet still creating significant strength and leadership in the DIY and contractor markets.

In 1995, Home Depot decided to investigate the possibility of opening stores in China. They selected several key vendors—of which we were one—to travel to Beijing—December 3–9—to meet with Home Way, headed by Mr. Du. The goal was to lay out the parameters for supporting the establishment of a retail big-box business. It was an interesting trip, and we met with several Chinese dignitaries and had the opportunity to explore Beijing. At the time, a city of bicycles—the principal mode of transportation—the roads were packed with them! A couple of stores did subsequently open, though the format did not match up with the Chinese culture, and eventually they were closed.

Jim Inglis retired from Home Depot in 1996 and most recently wrote a book, published in 2021, titled *Breakthrough Retailing: How a Bleeding Orange Culture Can Change Everything!* This book is a true and accurate recapitulation of the many sales and marketing programs successfully applied at Home Depot, many of which he initiated.

It is a wonderful book and, in great detail, identifies many techniques and strategies that he and other merchants used to successfully market the best home-improvement products at the most competitive prices to both contractors and homeowners. It is a must read for all retail operations irrespective of their product categories.

Baby Horsley—1939

Tony in Ashfield Avenue
garden—1947

Teenager Tony

Sebright School—Stanley Baldwin House
(Author—second row from front—third person from left—open jacket)

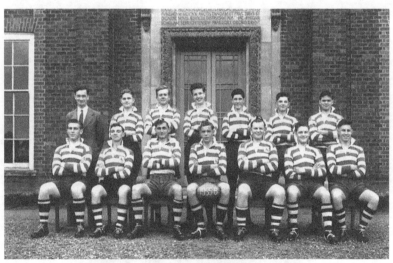

Sebright—Seven Aside Rugby Team Players
Author—Top row—far left next to coach.

Changing of the Colours—The Royal Warwickshire Regiment
(Author Front Left)

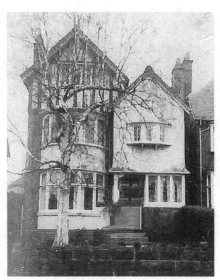

Author's Bimingham Home—Ashfield Avenue.

On Parade at Coventry Cathedral
Author Second from front (Saluting)

Officers of the Royal Warwickshire Regiment
Author center row, 6th from left

Author's Parents—Bill & Eve Horsley—1934

Author and his sister Susan—1944

Grandfather's Allotment—with my Mother
(Land rented to him for growing vegetables and flowers)

My father and I in our back garden

Author (right)—Tony Horsley, Best Man
at Martin Hoad's wedding

The Graham & Brown Team—Left to right—
George Root, John Carter, Tony Horsley, Roger
Graham, Mike Reilly, David Brown
Photographed in Blackburn, Lancashire, England

Author and his wife Susan

The Horsley Family (Back cover of book)

This picture shows Super Fresco textured wallpaper applied over paneling that has first been primed. In this case, a Wall Liner was applied over the primed paneling providing further assurance that the paneling grooves will be totally concealed when Super Fresco is installed.

Deck Restore Packaging

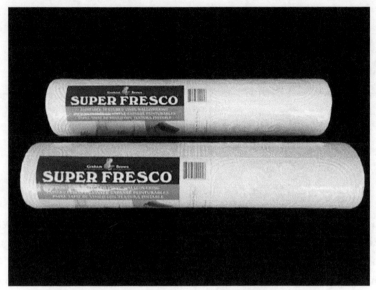

Super Fresco Paintable Textured Wallpaper Rolls

Ohio State Party Bus

22

The Nardelli Leadership

In 2000, there was a changing of the guard being considered with the possibility of CEO Bernie Marcus retiring. Ken Langone, the banker/investor who had largely established the initial funding for Home Depot, was now a board director. He was also on the board of General Electric. At the time of Jack Welsh's retirement from GE, Jeff Immelt was chosen as his successor, beating out another leading contender, Bob Nardelli. Langone believed that Nardelli would be an ideal CEO to step into Bernie Marcus's shoes, and this move took place in December of 2000.

This became the most disastrous event in the history of Home Depot. Nardelli had *zero* experience in retail and had ascended through the ranks of GE fostering a very different culture. Furthermore, he brought to Home Depot a questionable business strategy called Six Sigma. This is a process for improvement, principally in manufacturing, in which 99.99966 percent of opportunities to produce features of a part are statistically expected to be free of defects. It is a complex and ill-defined mythology, rarely if ever used, to manage and support retail operations.

Nardelli treated his employees and Home Depot stockholders with autocratic and critical style. In the process, he reduced costs, which damaged customer service, while competitor Lowe's was aggressively gaining market share. He was grossly overpaid and agreed to resign on January 3, 2007. His severance package was in

86

the region of $210 million. He was succeeded by the Home Depot vice chairman and executive vice president, Frank Blake, who calmed the waters and brought the company back to its original roots.

The real damage Nardelli inflicted was the exit and loss of many Home Depot superstar retail managers and executives. Truth was that most were millionaires, having benefited from the huge growth of their stock investments and options in the company. They were still working because they loved Home Depot, thrived on the business culture, and enjoyed the tremendous team effort they all contributed to.

From our standpoint, we did follow one of Nardelli's ill-fated actions. Historically Home Depot was organized and managed within regional divisions. Nardelli, favoring central control, changed this structure, and all stores were managed from the central headquarters in Atlanta. We—Mike and I—elected to follow suit and establish a national rep/service organization, WF Orr, who replaced the regional service organizations (previously discussed) around the country. This was a huge mistake, and in the shuffle, we lost much of the local control and service efficiency that was in place originally with the regional service groups. We never fully recovered the high level of service provided to the stores.

During this period, great talent was leaving the Home Depot merchandising and buying team. Thanks to Frank Blake and to his successor, Craig Menear, this tide of dissent has been corrected and reversed with Home Depot again leading the industry. At this point, in-stock wallcoverings were no longer offered and essentially concluded Graham & Brown's business activity in the United States.

Today there are very few retailers, including the big box stores, who still offer wallpaper for sale from in stock.

23

Meijer Thrifty Acres: Charlie Carpenter

Throughout the course of one's sales career, you may experience very diverse customer relationships—some great, and others not so great. Clearly Home Depot was a favorite. A well-managed entrepreneurial business led by an incredible army of merchants and operating people; every person you dealt with was totally focused on the customer. They were tough and demanding on their vendors in their quest to provide the best product/service and price for their customers.

Another great retailer was Meijer Thrifty Acres, headquartered in Grand Rapids, Michigan. They were a regional general merchandise chain with significant market strength, and we sold them our Glidden national brand paints. They also had a small private-label paint brand, and we decided to make a pitch for this business. The merchandising team we worked with was Harvey Lemmen, CEO; Harvey Kouche, merchandising manager; Ray Leach, VP of merchandising; and Dwight Shupe, paint buyer.

They were a great team to work with, and they all participated in every meeting we held. Clearly like most home-improvement/DIY retailers, paint was a critical and important category. We discussed with them our goal to present and sell a Meijer private-label brand. They were agreeable, and we scheduled a meeting.

Charlie, as usual, created a big board presentation—discussed earlier in this book—and we established the advertising commitment using sound data based on the volume we were generating with our national brand program. It was a powerful offering. I took possession of the presentation boards that Charlie had produced, with the plan to meet him at Cleveland Hopkins airport on the morning of January 21, 1976.

However, the evening prior, my wife, who was pregnant with our first child, received the warning of imminent delivery, and off to Fairview Hospital we ran! I called Charlie and met him at the airport early in the morning, delivered the presentation boards, and headed back to the hospital, happily in time to be present for the birth of our daughter Heather.

Meanwhile Charlie proceeded to Grand Rapids alone, apologized to the Meijer management team for my absence, and proceeded with the presentation—solo!

He explained my inability to join the meeting and said, "Gentlemen, I was born in Bad Axe, Michigan, and it is a pleasure to be back here today."

Mr. Lemmen, who had a speech impediment, said, "Charlie, I was born in Bad Axe too." Turning to his team, he asked the question, "Anyone else here from Bad Axe?" Silence. "Charlie," he said, "guess it is just you and I."

You will appreciate that because of Mr. Lemmen's impediment; whenever he spoke, his audience would remain very quiet and attentive, necessary to hear and understand his words. Such was the case on this occasion.

This set the scene for Charlie's presentation; it was very well received and unanimously approved and committed to. This new business acquisition roughly doubled our business volume from three to six million dollars, annually. The best lesson from all this is if you can present to all the *key decision-makers* and have the top dog present—in this case Harvey Lemmen—your chances of success are greatly enhanced! Furthermore, it fully substantiated the fact that Charlie Carpenter was the very best salesman on the Glidden team!

The program and marketing support we subsequently provided significantly increased their paint department volume and profitability, and that of Glidden also!

Our relationship with this retailer and its merchandisers became very close. We worked together to make the ingredients create significant sales gains.

Furthermore, we became good friends, and every twelve months or so, we would all get together to review business and socialize. It became an annual productive work and social partnership when we met. The first of which included an Ohio State and Michigan football game. Later when I moved to Toronto to run our Canadian operation, we had a get-together in that great city. These types of customer relationships are unique and add pleasure to one's business.

24

Citizenship

On January 6, 1999, I obtained my Certificate of Naturalization and became an American citizen, more specifically a dual citizen, with the ceremony taking place in Atlanta. It was a wonderful event shared with some three dozen other immigrants taking the Oath of Allegiance.

We all had the opportunity to speak and identify our journey to becoming a citizen. I included the fact that for me, it was some thirty-one years since I had originally come to the United States. A lady who spoke after me responded that she had originally immigrated some thirty-five years ago, thereby claiming the record within our group for time lapse from entry to naturalization!

25

Keller Williams: The Horsley Team

With the wallpaper business behind me, the next challenge emerged with encouragement from a friend and neighbor who was a very successful Keller Williams real estate agent, Trudy Provo.

She was a top performer with this entrepreneurial-focused company that fosters and supports organic growth. Simply described, a KW sales agent can recruit others to join KW (after first getting their real estate license if they were new to the business), and these recruited agents will become a part of their downline.

This provides the recruiting agent with a percentage of the commission earned by their new salesperson when they initiate and close a real estate transaction. This money comes directly from KW and is not funded by the selling agent—a win-win scenario! One is encouraged to recruit multiple agents, thereby magnifying their downline commissions.

If, as often is the case, their downline agents also recruit new agents, commissions will flow—at a lower percentage—from them also. The real jewel of the program is that when you move to another real estate firm and/or retire from KW, you will continue to receive these commission payments, so long as the applicable agents in your downline are still actively engaged in the business, working for KW in sales or buy activities.

Furthermore, when you die, these same commissions continue to flow to your designated beneficiary! This program is so rewarding financially that there are many KW agents whose business model focuses on building a large downline. I have been retired from KW for the past twelve years, and I still receive occasional automatic deposits in my checking account from the downline I originally created!

With this as background, my wife and I decided to get our real estate license; you cannot legally operate without this. We signed up and participated in a sixteen-week Barney Fletcher school. It was a great learning and fun experience. The participants were made up of men and women aspiring to become Realtors, with most either from or planning to join different real estate companies.

The best part were the instructors; all were seasoned real estate agents, and each one managed to weave into their curriculum, stories of wild and unusual experiences they have had during their real estate career. It was the most intriguing and fun schooling we have ever experienced!

With the course completed and the exam license passed, we were ready to rock and roll. An agent really has three road maps to follow: operate as a home-buyer's agent, a home seller's agent, or a combination of both. As a newcomer to the business, you take whatever you can get!

Our first client owned a back-split home that his sister was living in. He was a family friend and gave us the listing. There were a couple of challenges: His sister did not keep the house neat and tidy for showings. The second issue was that this back-split home was built so that to get into the house from the garage, you had to climb a steep flight of steps from inside the garage that took you up to the kitchen. There were a couple of finished rooms adjacent within the garage.

Our broker warned us that back-split homes are among the most difficult to sell! As luck would have it, the home sold quickly, and close to the asking price. After the closing, I asked the buyer what most appealed to him in selecting this home to buy. He told me he was a drummer, and every evening when he returns home from an engagement, he has a huge array of drums and cymbals to unload from his car and carry into his current apartment. This house that he has just purchased has a finished room adjacent and within the garage.

"Ten minutes max is what it now takes me to unload my gear with his new house!" he stated. This supports the oft-stated belief that there is a buyer for every house out there!

We continued as agents for three years, enjoyed it a great deal, particularly working with younger first-time buyers. Most liked and trusted us as they made what is likely one of the largest investments of a lifetime. We quickly learned that many viewed us as quasi parents, committed to helping them make the best buying decisions at a reasonable and fair price, with no surprises!

One final word on this business: there is good money to be made! Typically a listing agent will most often sell the property in conjunction with a buyer's agent who is representing the buyer. In which case, they will share the commission, which typically is 6 percent, so each will receive 3 percent at closing. It must be noted that the agent's broker gets a portion of the commission, and there will be some deductions for marketing and advertising costs. A $600,000 home sale will yield a $36,000 commission—$18,000 to each agent *less* the aforementioned expenses.

In some cases, the listing agent might also act on behalf of the buyer; in which case, they would earn the full $36,000, again, less the expenses. Commission percentages are sometimes negotiable between the agent and the homeowner.

We retired from our real estate adventure early in 2009. It was fast becoming a full and demanding business. At seventy years of age, I needed to slow down a little, which I did for a short time—well, for a couple of months.

26

Synta, Clarkston, Georgia: Tom Curtis, Dana Curtis, Randy Moore, Judy Moore

This next chapter discusses and identifies Randy Moore, an individual who had a significant influence and participation in my career and was highly skilled and focused on home decor.

In 1986, we met in Atlanta, when I was a salesman representing Norwall, and he was representing FSC Wallcoverings (F. Schumacher) and selling product, as was I, to the Home Depot. He was a powerful salesman and had a significant command of the industry. In 1993, he was hired by Home Depot as their Midsouth merchant, responsible for the procurement and marketing of both paint, paint sundries, and wallcoverings. In 1998, he was promoted to global product merchant, overseeing the worldwide sourcing of these categories.

He worked alongside and in conjunction with Home Depot regional paint merchants: Doug Craig > John Hanlon, Northeast; Dawn Foley > Cindy Prest, Florida; Steve Bebis > Dennis Johnson > Montsy Stelljes, Midsouth; Ernest Bidu, Southwest; Ron Carnes > Kim Curtin, West; Jim Shalda, Midwest.

As earlier narrated, I was selling Graham & Brown wallcoverings to all these divisions and had Randy's support from the Atlanta headquarters. He was a strong advocate of in-stock wallcoverings and helped me expand my sales initiatives throughout all the divisional buying offices.

In 2003, he left Home Depot and joined Synta Paint, a small Atlanta paint manufacturer owned and operated by Tom Curtis, who was previously the technical director at Camco Paint in Decatur, Georgia. Camco was originally owned and operated by Randy's godfather, Tom Campbell. Their two wives, Dana Curtis and Judy Moore, also worked at the Synta factory taking care of the accounting and administrative functions.

Tom Curtis was a skilled chemist and had developed a coating ideal for decorating and protecting wooden decks. The product contained significant quantities of sand aggregate designed to fill the cracks and gaps often inherent in aging decks. While Tom's technical skills focused on coatings technology, he was not a sales or marketing guru—hence his decision to hire Randy as his president, also vesting him in an ownership position of the company. They named the unique coating Deck Restore.

In March of 2009, Randy phoned and asked me to join Synta as a consultant and salesman. On my first day on the job, I arrived at the warehouse/plant in Clarkston, Georgia, asked the receptionist for Randy Moore, and was directed to the warehouse.

In this vast space, there was Tom and Randy standing on a large wooden deck that had been specially produced for the purpose of testing Deck Restore. It was a total disaster; they were both using a conventional lambswool roller cover to apply the coating. Problem was that as they rolled the coating onto the deck, the sand aggregate was being dispersed on top of the wood decking in an *extremely uneven* manner.

The finished appearance looked horrible! I asked myself, "What in the world am I getting into? This product is just not commercially viable."

Driving home that evening, I deliberated on the problem; the sand aggregate in the coating was being pushed and unevenly distributed because of the use of a smooth nap roller cover. Perhaps there was a different type of roller cover that might apply the sandy coating evenly?

I stopped at a Home Depot and examined their roller covers. I purchased a few "maybe" candidates and took them home for testing; none produced different or better results.

Continuing the search, the following week, I came across a garage floor coating that was being sold by a small independent paint retailer in Atlanta. The coating was manufactured in Toronto, Canada. Interestingly they also supplied a special roller cover that the paint store owner told me was important because this floor paint "contains a fine aggregate." I jumped at the mention of *aggregate*.

"How many roller covers do you have?" I asked.

"Six."

"I'll take them all!"

Back at home, I tested the roller cover—it was perfect and applied the Deck Restore coating thick and *evenly*. Today, seventeen years later the very same roller cover, web construction remains in use. See Appendix 4 "Restore Roller and Original Synta Deck Restore Press Release."

We now had a great deck coating and an applicator that worked. We were off to the races. Our first customer presentation was ACE Hardware, headquartered in Chicago.

ACE is a buying, marketing, and merchandising organization that supports some five thousand independent ACE Hardware stores across the United States. Randy and I flew to Chicago, having secured a meeting with their buying, advertising, and marketing team. We were able to use a huge room in our hotel for our presentation, and on our way in, we spotted and secured an old and battered wooden pallet in the parking lot.

We quickly "borrowed" the pallet and set it in the meeting room in readiness for our afternoon presentation. After lunch, we returned to the room—the pallet had disappeared. Turns out one of the hotel staff treated it as trash and took it to a huge outdoor dumpster! We quickly recovered it and returned it to the meeting room.

When our presentation began, we encouraged all the buyers and merchandisers to move in close and watch the demonstration. The pallet was a mess, severely cracked, dirty, and stained! Perfect! Using our recently acquired Restore Roller, we applied a thick coat of

Deck Restore, which quickly filled all cracks and distortions. It literally looked like a newly painted pallet when we finished—to rounds of applause.

Flying back to Atlanta, we knew for sure that we had a winning product. It was ready for market, and it could be tinted to a wide range of deck colors.

Shortly after the meeting, ACE asked us to participate in their upcoming national dealer trade show; we were invited to showcase and demonstrate Deck Restore in their innovation center. This provided us with significant exposure to the many independent ACE retailers attending the show. It was a great event, with the cumulative sales volume we achieved was in excess of a million dollars.

With this exposure and our confidence in the product, we quickly expanded our sales effort with other major retailers such as Home Depot, Menards, and Lowe's. We had a unique product and the wherewithal to quickly expand our distribution. Supporting the increased capital needs of such expansion, Synta needed additional funding and began to look for investors.

Happily Rustoleum, a major specialty coatings manufacturer headquartered in Chicago, acquired Synta in October 2012. Randy and Tom remained to manage the business, as did I, to continue selling and servicing customers throughout the USA.

The chemistry of the product originated and was maintained in the Synta Lab. Dat Vu, the technical director, managed the ongoing technical aspects and was closely overseen by Randy. The formula was, on occasion, slightly tweaked in order to refine and improve the product performance. Our sales continued to gain momentum and was notably improved when Home Depot rolled out the program to all their stores.

Early in 2010, sales were approaching the $50-million level, and then out of nowhere, we started to experience a slow and steady number of customer complaints.

These were, for the most part, characterized by the coating cracking and delaminating from the wood decking surfaces. We were quick to investigate and soon identified that for the most part, the failures were being caused by the lack of adequate preapplication preparation. We could tell that in most cases, the decks had not been first cleaned to remove algae, dirt, and prior stain or painted coatings.

Concurrent with our customer field investigations and remediations, the complaints magnified, and with threat of a class-action suit on the horizon, we hired Chicago law firm Meyer & Meyer to support our efforts.

Overnight my role at Synta changed from that of a salesman to becoming a technical arbitrator and a complaint handler. Lori Lightfoot—currently the mayor of Chicago, at the time, an attorney working for Meyer & Meyer—joined myself and Randy on many complaint calls helping to identify the root causes, provide solutions and remedial actions.

This was a very challenging time; we were committed to helping our customers achieve satisfaction with their deck refinishing. We provided replacement product and guidance on the best preparation methods; though many customers were angry and unhappy.

One customer phoned Frank Blake, who at the time was CEO of Home Depot, to register their dissatisfaction. Frank called Randy, and the next day, he and I were on a plane to Texas.

The initial challenges lasted close to a year during which time, the product formulation was changed to significantly improve adhesion. In the final analysis, the class-action suit was avoided, and Synta settled the case out of court. Since this time, Tom retired in 2012, and Randy moved forward as a consultant in 2015. He currently works exclusively as a consultant for M&A opportunities. I retired on October 12, 2016. Synta today continues as a successful and profitable coatings manufacturer under the ownership, direction, and leadership of Rustoleum.

27

Distinctive Wallcoverings & Decor

The next business venture evolved in 2017 when my good friend and former business associate at Graham & Brown, Bill Woods and I decided to market digital wallcoverings.

While the conventional wallpaper business in the USA was in serious decline, there was a growing interest and demand for custom one-off production of digitally produced wallcoverings. These products, unlike the conventional wallpaper we sold in the past, were custom printed on highly sophisticated HP digital printers, in small room lot quantities, as designated and required by the customer.

They were more expensive and vastly superior in quality to conventional wallpaper. As an example, reprinting the same design at a future date would always be a perfect color and design match. Not so with conventional wallpaper, where batch numbers were used to segregate productions.

We approached Parallax, an Atlanta digital printer, owned and operated by David Clevenger. They had a state-of-the-art facility crammed full of digital printers, all of which inspired us to create a business model supporting this product.

David was a successful entrepreneur, and clearly his high-end printing business was a masterpiece. We met and provided details of our wallcovering background and followed up with a detailed business plan identifying how we could launch and drive a significant wall decor business.

We registered and trademarked our business as Distinctive Wallcoverings & Decor. The first key task was to create a website, one that would physically manage and control the business flow, connected seamlessly to Parallax so that customer orders could reach them electronically for immediate production and shipment.

This was a major challenge for Bill and me, two guys who had no technical website competence in this field! We hired a small website designer located in Gainesville, Georgia, called Yapaweb, owned and operated by Martin Carrion. He provided the road map to creating a website, and we developed the pages, illustrations, and product definitions and characteristics. All these he used to complete the construction of the site.

The website was terrific, and we had high expectations of a significant volume of business. It did not happen! The simple fact is that we did not have the funds nor the wherewithal to use *social media* necessary to drive would-be customers to our website. The business failed as a result!

While this business is no longer active, we continue to host the site for the memory of it. You can visit the website by typing it into your computer browser, www.distinctivewalldecor.com, or use your mobile phone to scan the QR below.

DistinctiveWallcoverings & Décor

The site works as it did originally; the only difference is that if you try and place an order, nothing happens! You can search for wallpaper and murals and even use the global search box to view places of interest, anywhere in the entire world! The site, as we designed it, functions—even the tabs: products, order, installation, FAQs, blog, contact, and search. Check all this out, and you will see that digitally printed wallcoverings really are unique.

The lesson here is that if you have a good product to sell and use *only* your website as a sales vehicle, you will likely fail! You *must* use the powers of social media (TikTok etc.) to tell the world your story and bring would-be customers *to* your website! Not having the funds and wherewithal to embrace and use social media, the business will most likely fail as ours did!

At some point in the future, there is a plan to fund this business and relaunch it using the very same website and manufacturing platform.

28

Newport Clear Ice

In February 2018, while vacationing in the Dominican Republic, my wife and I met and became friends with Jonathan and Laura Daley, who were visiting from Connecticut. We planned to get together again to holiday in Newport, Rhode Island.

In September 2019, they picked us up at the Providence airport, and we drove to the Marriott, Rhode Island. We had a great visit, thoroughly enjoyed their company and the beauty of Newport. Jonathan works for a large corporation and, like me, has an entrepreneurial streak! He had brought with him a cooler of clear ice and described to me the freezing process.

Typically when water freezes, it becomes somewhat cloudy due to the mineral impurities and air bubbles that are retained in the ice tray. Not a pretty sight in your glass!

The solution is simple: Using a 3/8" round hollow hole punch, create a hole in the bottom of your ice trays. Place the trays supported in the top of a cooler and fill it with water to the upper level of the trays, then place in a freezer for thirty-six to forty hours. When you dispense the frozen cubes from the tray, they will be completely clear!

The secret to the process is downward directional freezing. The tap water you use is made to freeze from the top down, pushing most all the impurities and air bubbles through the precut holes in the bottom of the ice cube tray, leaving the clear ice on top in the tray!

We believe that the looks of one's refreshment are almost as important as the taste, so we decided to create a brochure designed to promote clear ice! We named it Newport Clear Ice. The lead page follows together with the detailed productions process. Scan the QR code or access the URL.

Newport Clear Ice Production Instructions
QR Code and URL

https://drive.google.com/
file/d/1biFMgU61PU1zefov9inb-tgsNIMGbQxc/view

29

Social Media: The Importance and Necessity of Using It in Marketing

This chapter will describe current social media characteristics and how they can support your business. Also provided below is a simple formula for converting a website or video URL to a QR barcode, used throughout this book.

The relatively new term *social media* has only been widely used in the last few years and is described by Google as follows: "Social Media are interactive technologies that facilitate the creation and sharing of information, ideas, interests and other forms of expression through virtual communities and networks."

The most popular major platforms for social media are Facebook, Twitter, LinkedIn, Instagram, Snapchat, TikTok, Pinterest, Reddit, YouTube, and WhatsApp—all of which one can use as sales generating and communication vehicles.

Each platform is measured by their number of monthly active users. This, at the time of writing, those listed above range from 2.7 billion to 310 million *per month*! Your goal is to develop as many followers for your products as possible.

My daughter Heather, as an example, has about sixty thousand on Instagram and about the same number on TikTok. Katy, a family friend, has some six hundred thousand followers, providing a huge sales audience.

As a brand marketer, you need the ability to connect directly with your prospects and develop partnerships with other online platforms, helping to grow both your and their brands.

The most effective way of doing this is through and with the support of other marketers, who ideally are selling similar product categories. These working associations are often referred to as "influencers."

With these social media influencer connections, you can build brand awareness, generate new leads/sales, and build brand authenticity. Best described as influencer marketing, which will help to generate significant growth for your online sales and exposure.

The influencer collaboration, supporting compatible online products or services, derives value and reinforcement for both your and their social media initiatives. Simply stated, influencers can generate brand awareness, resulting in added sales for all the participating parties.

Heather is an aggressive influencer and, on occasions, will purchase products from social media platforms and then create a TikTok video featuring the product in use. She will then post the video (at no cost) on her own platforms, receiving a commission on all sales thereby generated.

Her ability to create snappy and effective TikTok videos is well known, and this is becoming rewarding, most often with free product donations! View her TikTok video by typing this link into your browser—https://vm.tiktok.com/TTPdSeJKY5/—or scan the barcode.

TikTok

In chapter 27, when describing the failure of Distinctive Murals & Decor, I said that if you have a good product to offer using *only* your website as a sales and marketing vehicle, you will likely fail!

This is where social media takes over and is an *essential* ingredient enabling you to reach the masses, communicating that your product is readily available and can be seen, understood, and purchased on your website!

To summarize: your social media should create interest and excitement for your products, driving potential customers to your website, where they can purchase your product or service.

30

Our Children

This chapter is not designed to cheer the accomplishments of our two daughters. No question, I am proud of them both, their husbands, and my seven grandchildren. In many respects, they both exhibit entrepreneurial traits and have achieved some significant milestones and successes in life thus far. As of this writing, their ages: Heather is forty-seven, born in Cleveland, Ohio; and Holly is forty-two, born in Toronto, Canada.

Holly, while at Vanderbilt University, participated in a study-abroad program in Florence, Italy, for one semester in her junior year. Arriving in Florence on Monday, September 3, 2001. A week later, while sharing an apartment with classmates, 9/11 occurred. This was a challenging period for us as parents and for Holly and her class-mates living in a large European city.

A month after the attack, Sue and I flew to Florence and spent a week providing moral support for all and enjoyed lots of partying! We also visited Capri and Positano and concluded the trip in Venice, where Holly joined us for a much-needed respite. Following gradu-ation, she moved to Charlotte, bought a small and newly remodeled home, and worked for the local Coca-Cola bottling company.

From here, she joined Accenture as an analyst, where she met Kevin Harrell, and they married on November 10, 2007. She con-tinued her career working for R. T. Dooley, a leading Charlotte construction company. As a project manager, she became very popular with the management team, who affectionately renamed her Hollywood!

Today they have four children. Kevin is a great husband and father. He works for a private equity firm, Cerberus Capital Management. Holly manages the children (Holden, Carter, Brooks, and Evelyn), who all attend a nearby school. She also supervises the construction of their new home, discussed later.

Heather attended the University of Alabama in Tuscaloosa, and then attended grad school in Memphis, where she studied and became a certified speech and language pathologist. She met and married another Kevin, who, at the time, was working with me at Graham & Brown, the UK wallcoverings company. He currently works for DiversiTech, a leading manufacturer and distributor of household and commercial HVAC products and manages their key customers throughout North America.

Over the past ten years, Heather has created and established several very successful online businesses; the applicable websites are shown below:

- www.aglowpresets.com—A digital photo presets used in Adobe Lightroom enabling users worldwide to enhance their mobile phone photography, both stills and videos.
- www.aglowcandlecompany.com—An exciting range of candles, soaps, and room cleaning sprays sold direct to retail stores and homeowners throughout the USA.
- www.aglowbythesea.com (funded by the direct sales businesses mentioned above)—Rental properties she has purchased in the Florida Panhandle.

She continues her speech therapy, working for Presence Learning, with her area of responsibility, Southern California School Districts, where she remotely teaches and helps children with speech and language impairments.

They have three children: Maddy, who has just finished her second year at the University of SC; Lawton, eighteen, will be attending Presbyterian College in South Carolina on a football scholarship, with a starting date of August 2023; Hyatt, at fifteen years, is also into football and is not yet ready to make the big choice! Of note, he is a superlative fisherman!

Heather's Kevin is also a great husband and father. Indeed, both sons-in-law are closely woven into our family; we love them and are proud of them both. In addition, we have become good friends with both their parents, who are super great people, Sue and Chuck Cox and Chris and Ronnie Harrell.

Heather's websites can be accessed using the QR barcodes below:

www.aglowpresets.com

www.aglowcandlecompany.com

www.aglowbythesea.com

31

Meritable Mentions

In the following sections, I have narrated some of the important and relevant achievements of friends, my brother-in-law, and business acquaintances.

Lynette Jennings

A nationally renowned designer and trusted authority of decor, design, and producer of House Smart, was hired as a consultant by Home Depot in 1994. She brought to their retail stores decor and design credibility and added strength to their decorating and "softer" side of the business.

As a wallcoverings supplier, we were delighted with her appointment and worked directly with her, helping to reinforce the decor side of Home Depot's hard-line image. We introduced Lynette to the Graham & Brown owners, David and Roger. She became a relevant decor reinforcement and added strength, supporting our goal of developing the decor business in a male-oriented hard-lines environment.

On April 27, 1999, together with Lynette, we traveled to New York to meet with a candidate advertising agency. With time to spare after the meeting, I took our party to the New York Stock Exchange for a tour. It was a particularly memorable event, as a month earlier, the DOW had closed over $10,000 for the first time in history!

On March 29, to be exact. Passing through the gift shop as we left, they were selling "DOW $10,000" caps, manufactured by the New England Cap Company. I purchased one for all of us!

As an avid participant in the stock market, this was a momentous occasion, and I decided to continue the tradition of purchasing caps for my personal group of friends who were in the market. As each future key benchmark was achieved—$15,000; $20,000; $25,000; and $30,000—I had caps produced (inscribed with the applicable dollar benchmark) and sent to this select group of fifteen friends/investors. At this point, $30,000 is the most recent cap commemoration. Here is the chart that supported this event and includes each date the DOW achieved the milestone:

Date	DOW $ Value	Time frame
Tuesday, May 26, 1896	$40.94	First day of the DOW
Tuesday, November 21, 1995	$5,023.55	99 years and 8 months later
Monday, March 29, 1999	$10,006.78	3 years and 5 months later
Tuesday, May 7, 2013	$15,055.90	14 years and 1 month later
Thursday, February 24, 2017	$ 20,810.32	3 years and 9 months later
Thursday, January 4, 2018	$ 25,075.13	1 year later
Tuesday, November 24, 2020	$30,046.24	2 years later
Friday, July 23, 2021	$35,061.55	8 months later

Bryan Langton

In 1990, ahead of David and Roger's upcoming visit to Atlanta, Roger called me from the UK to ask a favor. "I have an old school pal, his name is Bryan Langton, and I believe he is now working at the Atlanta Holiday Inn, close to Perimeter Mall. Could you please contact him and see if we can get together for lunch one day during our upcoming visit?"

A simple-enough request! Problem was I had no idea what Bryan did—was he a busboy, front-desk manager, or whatever? So I called the hotel and asked for Bryan Langton; eventually I was put through to a secretary who told me that he was in Paris, at a board meeting!

I explained the circumstances of my call, and she agreed to set up a lunch meeting on his return from Europe and when David and Roger were in Atlanta. Turns out, he was the worldwide Holiday Inn CEO.

The day arrived, and we met at the dining room at the Holiday Inn and were joined by Bryan. A very personable individual with a strong British accent. After the pleasantries, we asked how as the CEO of Holiday Inn, he chose Atlanta as his US headquarters.

The story is as follows: After his appointment as CEO, he was directed by Bass (the UK Brewery and owner of Holiday Inn) to visit their USA headquarters, which, at the time, was in Memphis, Tennessee. Bryan and his wife flew to this city via Atlanta, where they overnighted before traveling to Memphis the following day. After a day in Memphis, both he and his wife decided that (a) they were not too keen on Memphis as a headquarters city, and (b) Atlanta, as a major international hub city, represented a more suitable headquarters for Holiday Inn.

On their return to the UK, they stopped again in Atlanta for a couple of days and met with city officials—all of whom enthusiastically offered significant financial incentives designed to capture the Holiday Inn headquarters for their city. Little did they realize that a decision in favor of Atlanta had already been made! Atlanta became the North American home for Holiday Inn and remains so today.

Our luncheon continued with stories relating to the hospitality business and, from our side, discussions about the retail home-improvement markets focused primarily on Home Depot.

Bonnie Rothman Fitch

I first met Bonnie in 1998, in Atlanta; she was dating entrepreneur Ned Fitch, and I met up with them both in Café Tu Tu Tango, a fun Buckhead restaurant and watering hole! They had bought a home nearby, the very same thirteen-home enclave that my wife and I had just also purchased a home—we were neighbors.

Bonnie worked for Home Depot as an import merchant and, in fact, was the very first such merchant hired into Home Depot, responsible for global product sourcing. She led the initial sourcing efforts for THD when Mainland China opened up, and had the ability to work directly with factories in China began.

She was eminently qualified, being a talented negotiator and able to speak fluent Mandarin Chinese. Prior to joining Home Depot, all their imports were done indirectly through Taiwanese trading companies, who, at the time, tried to control the Chinese factories themselves and block them from selling direct to US retailers.

She had studied, lived, and worked in both Mainland China and Taiwan and therefore was able to exercise unique insights into working with the Mainland Chinese and Taiwanese and advise Home Depot management on entering business ventures in the Far East.

Petite with red hair and good looks, she did not exactly fit the image of a tough, demanding, sourcing merchant. So much so that on one occasion, when meeting with a major barbecue manufacturer, she listened intently as their manufacturing chief opened the discussions in his native language that translated to, "We could sell anything to this customer because Americans don't know anything about quality. We have an opportunity to sell products to them at irrational and high prices, and we don't need to worry about enforcing product specifications or any quality standards!"

Bonnie, of course, understood every word he had spoken, to the point that he was deeply shocked when she responded in fluent Chinese that the meeting was immediately terminated! The moral of this story is never take for granted your supplier's ability or potential to misrepresent and outwit you!

Home Depot pioneered the most stringent quality assurance programs in support of all their worldwide imports. When manufacturers saw how serious they were about quality, their compliance quickly followed. They were also one of the first major retailers to enforce the nonuse of child and prison labor by their suppliers.

Bonnie's husband, Ned, and I became good friends, and with our neighborhood still being developed, we formed a homeowner's association designed to ensure ongoing construction compliance from the builder/developer, Mike Landry. Additionally we set up the necessary covenants and restrictions to ensure consistency and homeowner guidelines.

Ned owned and managed a successful coffee and tea import business that he had created called Kalahari, while Bonnie traveled the world, sourcing and developing product opportunities and private-label product for Home Depot.

One of the products that she sourced was a unique folding worktable which Ned and I saw as an ideal DIY product for the USA. We developed a marketing and packaging plan designed to sell the table to craft and hobby enthusiasts. We even made a trip to Bentonville, Arkansas, and attempted to sell the table to Walmart; they had buying offices in China and could source such a product without our help!

We remain friends to this day, where they still live in their Buckhead house, which has been renovated and beautifully updated many times.

Mike Bell

Mike, my brother-in-law and a wonderful friend, who you will earlier recall that it was at his wedding that I met my wife, Susan, his sister!

Mike was born February 29, 1948, in Cleveland, Ohio. He joined the United States Marine Corps in 1966 and served courageously in Vietnam, attaining the rank of sergeant, earning both a Purple Heart and a Bronze Star. During this period, he survived a direct hit in his helicopter from enemy fire, which crashed to the ground.

Mike enjoyed a successful career with Foseco Metallurgical Inc., spanning thirty-five years, supporting the sales and marketing of their metallurgical products in New York, Texas, and Virginia, managing their sales regions.

Earlier in his career, he was involved in their production of brake linings and would recount how he was continually exposed to asbestos in the production facility. Unhappily this probably contributed to his death resulting from mesothelioma at the age of fifty-nine.

His most avid and favorite pursuit was that of supporting the Ohio State University football and basketball teams, season after season! He was, by any measure, a true and fanatical Buckeye.

He once invited me to meet in Columbus, Ohio, for us to attend an Ohio State versus Northwestern football game. Having been schooled in the UK and played rugby, my grasp of college football at the time was very limited; plus I was *not* ready for the "fever" of Ohio State football!

I arrived the night before at the Columbus airport and was escorted to several local bars where we met with his drinking buddies; the sole topic of conversation was the need for Ohio State to beat Northwestern the following day.

That evening, as we parted for our hotel rooms, Mike said, "We will be meeting in the lobby tomorrow at 6:00 a.m."

"Six a.m.?" I retorted. "The game does not start until 1:00 p.m.!"

"Be there at six—that's when we start tailgating," he replied. I was too embarrassed to ask what "tailgating" was!

I was soon to find out! Ouch! We arrived at a large parking area just outside the stadium that was filled with hundreds of decorated vehicles—many painted bright red, the Buckeye's color. Mike had very close friends, Terry and Retta Russell, who live in Columbus, Ohio. They had purchased an old school bus and had it professionally converted, and added the insignia, "The Ohio State Buckeyes—2002 National Champions." See photo on Page 85. This was to be our home for the next ten hours or so!

I immediately spotted a black mat at the foot of the steps leading into the bus; it bore the Northwestern logo. I quickly discovered that this was for stomping on, thereby inflicting pain on the enemy!

Alcohol was flowing everywhere—vodka, gin, beer, wine, you name it. Grills were set up and breakfast was being served! I can honestly say that I have never experienced such levels of enthusiasm, perhaps better described as a cult following!

The football game was an incredible event also, and happily Ohio State won—more alcohol and more celebrating. The following day, I was poured onto my flight back to Atlanta, just a little hungover!

Following his death on April 13, 2007, we hosted a celebration of life in Nellysford, adjacent to the Wintergreen, Virginia, resort where Mike lived. A burial service was held at Arlington National Cemetery on his sixtieth birth date, February 29, 2008. This was a wonderful and moving military event, which you can view by typing the URL https://youtu.be/YhVBAiOKuGA into your computer browser, or use your mobile phone to scan the barcode below.

Mike Bell, Arlington National Cemetery

Bob Douglas/Berkshire Hathaway

In 1998, when we moved into our Buckhead home, we made immediate friends with Bob and Diane Douglas. Their home was directly across the street from ours, which later proved to be an asset when frequently partying back and forth between both!

Bob was an owner/principal of an investment firm—Bey/Douglas—and a skilled investor/money manager, so with both our interest and participation in the stock market and love of partying, helped to quickly promote a close friendship.

We spent vacations and traveled together often. Probably the most memorable was when Bob and I journeyed to Omaha, Nebraska, to attend the Berkshire Hathaway stockholders meeting. To say this was a momentous and exciting event would be a gross understatement!

Warren Buffet and his business partner, Charlie Munger, are brilliant stock pickers. They have invested heavily in many leading and diverse companies and banks, which they view as long-term, solid, and predictable income producers.

Historically they have shied away from some categories they deem as high risk, such as technology companies. Recognizing this, back in 2010 and 2011, they hired Todd Combs and Ted Weschler respectively; both were very successful mutual fund operators. Their role at Berkshire—stock pickers. One of Weschler's early moves was to buy Apple stock, and as of this writing, this investment tops $150 million and is by far Berkshire's largest holding.

Bob and I flew to Omaha, rented a car, and drove to our hotel in Council Bluffs, Iowa. There were no hotel rooms available in Omaha anywhere close to the convention center. Seems the Omaha hotels were completely sold out way ahead of the Berkshire event.

Adjacent to the huge auditorium (where the actual stockholders meeting is held each year) was a convention hall filled to the brim with booths displaying products of most all the Berkshire companies. It was just like the trade shows that I was accustomed to attending at the Chicago McCormick Convention Center!

Seats at the meeting are not preallocated, and while we were high up, had a great view of the desk at which Warren and Charlie were sitting and answering questions. Q and A is the format of the meeting; questions come from the floor, plus those documented and provided ahead of the meeting.

We also had a great view of the Berkshire directors and VIPs seated at the front of the meeting. Here we could see the who's who of corporate America. The meeting typically lasts five hours.

Once the meeting is over, shareholders are invited by Warren Buffet to visit the various Berkshire retail outlets in Omaha, and "Please spend your money," he urged! They keep a tally of the revenues derived during the stockholder's meeting period, which are very significant. We visited many of their retail stores, the largest two of which were a furniture store—Nebraska Furniture Mart—and Borsheims, an upscale jewelry store, where Warren was behind their counter selling to the swarm of customers!

Berkshire shares have grown significantly since the company's initial stock offering in 1939, so much so that the unit price became beyond the reach of most individual investors. This was changed by the conversion of original shares being designated as class A shares, along with the formation of class B shares, which have a face value of 1,500 times less. Today's class A shares are trading in the $559,000 range, and the class B shares can be bought or sold for about $370. Warren Buffet is reported to have no plans to split the Class A shares, as they are designed to attract long-term, high-quality buy-and-hold investors.

Without a doubt, Berkshire is a totally one-of-a-kind organization by *any* measure. Here's one more unique operating feature. Being a big player in the insurance business, they collect "premiums," money paid to them up front for security against loss, damage, and disasters. Berkshire calls this money *float*, and yes, they use it to purchase additional new businesses!

These two pages on Berkshire Hathaway are just a glimpse into the world of business and investing. If this whets your appetite, there are many great books to read. My favorite is *The Snowball: Warren Buffett and the Business of Life*, written by Alice Schroeder.

Diane, Bob's wife, meanwhile operated during this time a home design and building construction business, specializing in high-end properties that she built and sold in Bent Tree, a picturesque mountain community some sixty miles north of Atlanta. The final home she built was for themselves and where they moved from Buckhead to retire. We still get together often to party and recount our days in the big city.

32

Creating Wealth

This chapter and the next two discuss both wealth generation strategies, together with a few examples of missed opportunities! First a brief history of the financial growth of Home Depot and that of its two founders, Bernie Marcus and Arthur Blank.

Home Depot became a public company on September 22, 1981. The stock opened at $12 a share, traded on NASDAQ. Factoring in thirteen stock splits since the IPO, the split-adjusted IPO value per share in 2022 would be $0.02 per share.

If you invested just $1,000 at the IPO, you would have purchased eighty-three shares. Thanks to all the stock splits and share price appreciation, your investment would be valued today, close to $10 million, provided you sold none of your shares. That is creating wealth!

Along with many others at Home Depot, the founders became extremely wealthy (billionaires, to be exact) and remain so today. They have pledged to give to charitable causes a significant portion of their wealth. Evidence of their philanthropy is regularly reported, particularly in "their" city of Atlanta.

In addition to their generous wealth sharing, both have created Atlanta landmarks: Arthur Blank—The Falcons football team, Atlanta United Soccer team, and the Mercedes-Benz Stadium; Bernie Marcus: The Georgia Aquarium, Job Creators Network, and the

Marcus Foundation, providing, significant grants to many Atlanta area hospitals.

They both continue to share their wealth in Atlanta and beyond. Their generosity and commitment to the city in which they first launched Home Depot is unprecedented and wonderful.

33

Wealth Generation Strategies

Creating wealth is the ambition of many! By definition, *wealth* is best defined as the sum of your assets, less any debts you have.

Accomplishing wealth has several paths, some better and some riskier than others, and some just don't work! I make no promises; here are my ideas and experiences, beginning with a list of tactical guidelines:

a. Achieve a high level of college education—degree/MBA/doctorate.

b. Seek a unique and compelling business to work for.

c. Invest in the stock market.

d. Invest in Bitcoin.

e. Establish and create your own business.

f. Invest in real estate.

g. Develop an online business/marketplace.

h. Work/partner with a visionary entrepreneurial person or business.

i. In addition to stock portfolios, establish a savings account/plan

j. Use a budget to establish and manage your wealth-building plan.

k. Consider the use of retirement accounts such as 401(k) and Roth IRA.

l. Establish a pension plan, described in chapter 20.
m. Set up and fund a portfolio at the birth of each of your children and grandchildren. I use Schwab, which is an ideal vehicle for this. Keep funding! You will be amazed how quickly their wealth will accumulate!

I will comment on a few of these tactical guidelines:

a. A great education will always be a significant asset that will maximize your capabilities and opportunities for a lifetime.
b. Your background, interests, and exposure likely will provide you with the type of business you will find most rewarding. In my case, it was sales and decorative products. I always had a love for both and still do to this day!
c. Below are some of the principal stock market positions that I established about twenty-five years ago. When originally constructing the portfolio, I selected two companies that I believed would be the *principal drivers* over time: Home Depot and Apple. Both were led by terrific innovators, had great depth of management, and were very well-operated businesses.

   One other key ingredient was that they both believed in and executed stock splits on a regular basis. Together they represent some 34 percent of my total portfolio today, thanks to their superior performance.

   I show these positions along with their current percentage allocation in the total portfolio. This percentage is important and can greatly influence the overall gains (or losses).

   Cash (6.28), ACN (1.55), ABT (2.64), ADBE (2.70), AMZN (6.34), AAPL (18.22), BRK-B (6.93), DHR (6.18), HD (16.15), JPM (1.85), LEN (2.1), MSFT (9.75), NVDA (5.78), SHW (5.33), TSLA (5.11), TMO (3.09).

   I select from these stocks in order to create my grandchildren's portfolios. As time goes by and they reach their midteens, I show them their portfolio positions, together with the overall performance. Also I try to explain the market and the tremendous value of investing at a very early age. I ask that when they get jobs (even before, during, and after college), they also need to begin to join me in the funding process!

This is *not easy*! They look at the total dollars thus far accumulated, and their imaginations start spinning—"Can I get a new bike, Papa?" *No* is the firm answer! It will take time and patience to get them thinking long-term.

d. Bitcoin is not for the faint of heart! It does have the capacity for financial gain—be careful!

e. Establishing a new business from scratch is an exciting and rewarding exercise! Horsley Marketing Services (HMS Inc.) was my first, and more recently Distinctive Wallcoverings & Decor LLC.

My daughter Heather's three businesses are described in chapter 30, and yes, she has more planned for the future!

Once you have determined the product or service and how you plan to go to market, there is a process you will need to follow. First, register your company name as an LLC. All states require that every corporation, limited liability company, and limited partnership authorized to transact business in the state to file an annual registration. (The annual cost in Georgia is $150.)

You are now off and running. Here are some of the tasks you should follow:

1. Write a detailed business plan. All the intricate details are probably in your head, but this step is essential. Make this document as detailed as possible; it will become your road map as you establish and develop your operating format and strategy. In addition, your plan will be a useful tool when meeting with investors, suppliers, and prospective customers.

Listed below are the key topics you should incorporate:

Mission statement (state your personal business background together with the background of the business you plan to launch), competition, product characteristics, sourcing and distribution, financial objectives, pricing, branding (trademark), compelling competitive positioning/advantages, logistics/infrastructure, website strategy, management structure. Update your plan as necessary from time to time. Be sure to include your social media plan and strategy.

2. Establish and set up the necessary manufacturing needs for the products you are going to produce, market, and sell. Develop pricing and distribution elements.

3. If your plan is to source products from a third-party manufacturer, establish the details, pricing, product range, shipping, and warehousing, together with a sales and marketing plan. Make sure to establish a written agreement between the parties, specifying pricing, terms of sale, product ranges, complaint procedures, and inventory management.

4. Before you start to design your website, you should first establish a URL (uniform resource locator). This will be your website address, such as mine shown in paragraph 5. It must be unique to you and can easily be set up on line using Directnic; access their site at www.directnic.com. Click on the .com box (.com is way more frequently used than .net). Click on US domains and type in your preferred URL that best identifies your business—distinctivewalldecor describes my business well.

You will be provided with several options, particularly if your choice is currently in use, which of course you cannot use. Once you select the best option for your business, you can purchase it—cost is about $15, depending on the options you select. The site is very user friendly and simple to navigate.

5. The next big step will be the creation of a website. This requires considerable skill, and you may decide to hire a

professional web designer to do this for you. Also, they will be able to host the site when you are ready with product to go live.

Your website is an essential component supporting your business. This will become an information center for prospects, customers, and suppliers. Check out my website, previously discussed and added again below. Remember that it is hosted (active), so you can browse it, but you cannot make a purchase as it is no longer connected to a digital printer! You can visit the website by typing in your browser www.distinctivewalldecor.com, or scan the barcode below.

Distinctive Wallcoverings & Décor

6. Brand names, product specifications, letterheads, and business cards, along with any technical support literature will need to be developed. The creation of a smart logo is a must, such as:

Distinctive Murals & Decor

7. Finance—Any start-up business is going to need financial support from the beginning. Create a realistic budget and make sure you have the funds to fully cover (with a reserve) your business launch with a minimum of twelve months back-operating funds on hand.

8. Trademark registration—Your product brand name *must* be protected so that later when your business is well established, no one else will legally be able to use it. This does not need to be done until your business is established and

operational. Access the website at https://www.uspto.gov/trademarks, or scan the barcode below.

United States Patents and Trademark Office

However, you cannot use a trademarked name that already exists and is in use. The USPTO website will allow you to do a quick search to see if your brand/name is already in use. It is imperative that you conduct this research *before* establishing your product/brand name.

Click on the box Search (TESS). In the select and search option, click on Basic Word Mark Search (New User). In the box, enter the trademark you would like to register. Then click on "Submit Query." The site will identify if your trademark is already registered by someone else.

Here are the detailed and easy steps for you to register your trademark name. I use this company/website to begin the process, www.trademarkengine.com, or scan the barcode below. Click on "Get Started" and the application will populate. Answer all the questions, and I suggest for your first registration, you select the deluxe package ($199).

Once you have answered all the questions and transmitted the document, Trademark Engine will process the information you have provided and submit it to TEAS@ uspto.gov.

Shortly thereafter, you will receive a notification providing you with a serial number and confirming all information that the government examiner will be processing, including the completion timeline, which could be up to a year out!

One of the options is to include your website URL. While this is not mandatory, I suggest you do include, as this way, the USPTO examiner can see that you have a professional business you wish to trademark. The government filing fee is currently $350.

34

Missed Opportunities

You might imagine that with my close business relationship with Home Depot founders, Bernie Marcus and Arthur Blank, described earlier, that I would have jumped all over their IPO and invested every penny I had!

When this event took place on September 22, 1981, I was busy in Atlanta getting HMS off the ground, seeking manufacturers to represent. I was totally unaware of the IPO; this missed opportunity cost me a few million dollars for sure! On the plus side, my stock market investments detailed in chapter 33 have been very rewarding.

Other missed financial gains over the years were (in addition to THD's IPO) largely confined to real estate. I made money on the Great Exuma land I sold, but the remaining transactions were not impressive. Most were the result of selling property too soon and before significant appreciation had occurred.

The average sale price of houses sold in the USA from the early '80s to the present grew from some $50,000 to over $400,000 today. A gain of eight times!

The fact is that good, well-located real estate has, and likely will, always increase in value. Even today, real estate prices are going through the roof! Here is one example of my experience with the home I purchased when I first immigrated to Atlanta.

At the time, I was living in an apartment off Interstate 85, north of Atlanta, a two-lane freeway (at the time) leading into the city. I worked out of the Glidden paint store on Luckie Street in downtown, so whenever it rained, I had an extended commute of well over an hour. On one such occasion, I decided to search for a place to live closer to the city.

Druid Hills is directly to the east of downtown Atlanta, connected by Ponce De Leon Avenue—not heavily traveled, and an ideal location to commute from.

In 1969, I purchased a home on Lullwater Road, Druid Hills, Atlanta. Price, furnished—$35,000. I sold it in 1975 for $90,000. Today's value is about $1,300,000 and remains one of the least expensive homes on the street! Lullwater Road is a picturesque area lined with an abundance of dogwood trees and profuse azaleas. The road connects Ponce De Leon Avenue to Emory University and is lined with magnificent homes, set back from the road in immaculately landscaped gardens.

There is a beautiful park with Lullwater Creek flowing through, just steps away from my home, with a suspension bridge connecting several other paths in the park and which crosses a small lake. This beautiful area is not well known, with few visitors, and not many children come to play, so one can enjoy the tranquility and quietness. It was in this park that several years later, I proposed to my wife, Sue!

The house was not particularly attractive compared to other properties on the street. The price was affordable, and in the lower level, there were two separate apartments that were rented to Emory University students, which covered my mortgage payment! It was a perfect bachelor pad, and when my mother later immigrated to the USA, she lived in the house, concurrent with my transfer to Glidden's headquarters in Cleveland, Ohio. Location, location wise, this is by far the best real estate investment I have ever made!

There is one other factor you should consider when purchasing real estate and hoping to profit when selling later: comparative value to other nearby properties. My Lullwater Road house was among the least expensive homes on the street, with some properties, at the time, exceeding a million dollars! This scenario will often help to create more value when time comes to sell.

To this day, the Druid Hills Civic Association hosts a home and garden tour at the end of April each year that includes properties on Lullwater Road; my wife and I always attend and enjoy visiting the many beautifully decorated and landscaped homes. This activity certainly provides some additional value to the area and many of the houses.

The subsequent seven homes and two vacation houses we bought and sold over the years all provided profitable gains in value but were not individually that significant due to the short ownership time frame. The real gains materialize when one owns a property for a time frame of ten years or more!

One must be patient with any investment, particularly real estate, where the oft-used term is "Location, location, location." Simply stated, the intrinsic value lies not just in the home's construction, beauty, and excellence but rather in the quality of its location. You can tear down an ugly house and rebuild it, but you cannot change the location of the lot that you own and that the house sits on!

My younger daughter, Holly, lives in Charlotte with her husband and four children, discussed earlier. Their house is best described as "the money pit," as depicted in the movie bearing this name—a house that constantly was deteriorating and had many structural problems! They considered moving and building the house of their dreams. The builder they were working with told them, "You keep telling me how much you love your present location. For a slight increase in price, I can tear down your house and build a beautiful new one on your lot!"

Simple solution, and as of this writing, their house has been leveled, and a magnificent replacement is under construction. The only downside is that they had to move to a rental home for a year while their new house was being built. To view the demolition video, scan the QR code below:

House demolition

Bitcoin, another missed opportunity—This is not for the faint of heart! It is, however, a currency that is becoming relevant and more widely used. It is one of the first broadly accepted cryptocurrencies, and one of the best known. Summed up, it is digital money that functions outside normal banking practices and can be easily and safely transferred between both business and private parties.

A friend had their website hacked, and the perpetrator demanded a payment in Bitcoin, necessary to reinstate the site. I came to the rescue and transferred a small amount, and the site was immediately reinstated.

I purchased Bitcoin in the fall of 2017, at $2,967 per unit and sold it a year later with a modest profit. At the present time, its price is in the $26,000+ range. A very large missed opportunity! Visit www.bitcoin.com

35

North American DIY Retailers

This book discusses the principal North American DIY Retailers, both past and present that the author has worked and personally communicated with since he first immigrated to the United States in 1968. See list in Appendix 1. Several have ceased to operate. This represents a hundred plus home-improvement DIY operations in the United States and Canada.

The attrition rate is high and magnified by the significant growth, market leadership, and success of Home Depot, Lowe's, Menard, and ACE Hardware over the years.

Google searches were used in most all cases to identify and verify business closures. The author assumes no responsibility for the validity or accuracy of these closures. Possibly more closures could take place before the publication of this book!

Appendix 2 lists today's leading paint manufacturers.

36

On Safari

Adventure, animals, Africa, *Gateway to America* would not be complete without sharing an unbelievable safari adventure in South Africa.

The Safari web site URL is provided below.

Web site: www.brownandhudson.com

While the itinerary provides considerable detail of the trip, a brief recap is in order. First, to those readers who have never been on a safari, it is a must—add it to your bucket list! There are many companies you can go with and, of course, many destinations! Using a travel agency, as we did, is advisable, one that has had good experience in this field. They will guide you and provide the many location options.

South Africa is a great location for safaris. The "tented" description made us a little nervous, but as it turned out, the tents were quite luxurious, very comfortable, and safe!

The guides do all the driving; they are very professional and keep everyone in the vehicle safe. Their goal is, of course, to locate animals and get the vehicle as close as possible for us to photograph and experience animal nature at its best.

It amazed us that for the most part, *all* the animals generally ignored us and the Land Rover vehicles we were riding in! The reason is that safari tours have been taking place since their birth in the jungle, so what's the big deal!

Most often we would be on safari during the mornings, go back to our camp for lunch and a siesta, and then in the midafternoon, we would return. On occasions breakfast, lunch, or dinner would be set up in the jungle, where we enjoyed wonderful food.

For the most part, it was commonplace to see many animals, generally peaceful, playing in the sun.

We saw and photographed the "big five." These are referred to as the most difficult African mammals to hunt. They are the lion, leopard, rhino, elephant, and African buffalo.

We were very fortunate (so our guides told us) to encounter a pride of lions chasing and killing a buffalo. I was able to film the entire event, and if you scan the QR code below, you can watch the video. I offer caution if you cannot handle the killing of an animal. The video has been watched over seventy thousand times on YouTube.

Click on this URL or scan the QR code: https:// youtu.be/hBNULQcTUUI

The Lion's Prey—A Cape Buffalo

37

Moviemaking

Beginning many, many years ago, I was an avid moviemaker. Back then, the cameras were bulky, heavy, and used large VHS videotapes. I produced family movie events and played them back on television screens using VHS recorder/players. The video and sound quality of these devices, at best, was "fair."

Thanks largely to Steve Jobs and his Apple teams, today is a different story! You can of course buy professional high-tech video cameras, but with an iPhone, who needs them!

Apple, to a *large degree*, focuses on improved photo and video performance when launching new phone models each year. Here is their announcement heralding the 13 Pro:

<u>iPhone 13 Pro—Oh. So. Pro</u>

iPhone 13 Pro takes a huge leap forward, bringing incredible speed to everything you do and *dramatic new photo and video capabilities—* all in two great sizes.

They continually do an amazing job of measurably improving photographic quality with every new model phone they launch! This is what I use; it is always with me. At a moment's notice, I can shoot a video and/or still pictures. From the young to the old, we have become a nation of videographers! Speed, ease, quality, and convenience describe today's moviemaking. One can easily save raw/unedited videos and still pictures on your mobile phones, computers, and external storage devices.

Many of us go a step further, making slideshows and actual movies. Here are the tools you can use: (1) mobile phone, (2) Apple or PC computer, (3) movie software which is preloaded on Mac computers and many PCs.

Apple provides detailed instructions for enhancing your photos and video clips; plus they have good tutorials for making videos and slideshows. Here is a link to Apple's moviemaking guide: https://support.apple.com/guide/imovie.

This is the official iMovie instructions. There are also many websites available that support making videos on a PC.

In my early moviemaking days, I would burn my videos onto a DVD disk for playback and/or mailing it to friends and family. This step is no longer necessary! Set up your YouTube channel on your computer, then just upload the video or slideshow to your YouTube channel. Then e-mail the video link to friends and family.

Over the years, I have developed my own process for making movies and how to use YouTube to store and easily share movies with friends and family.

YouTube is a great video platform. I have over one hundred movies stored on my YouTube channel, all of which can be accessed from my iPhone and computer. One can control viewership by using these settings when e-mailing the video link to friends and family.

Private disallows access to movies from all, except those you have sent the video link to. Those who receive your link and forward to other people, *it cannot* be opened by others! For the most part, this is the setting I use.

Unlisted is similar to private, but if the recipient forwards the link to others, they, too, can view the movie.

Public—this setting allows any or all to access your video, even those who are surfing or searching on the web. I use this setting for some of my videos that are of general interest (example: Atlanta Botanical Gardens; see barcode and URL on next page).

https://atlantabg.org
Atlanta Chihuly Botanical Gardens

There is one other tool you may have a use for. I have many friends who have videos that are on old and obsolete tape formats and need to convert them to a current format or, better yet, transfer them to their computer hard drive or directly to their YouTube library channel. Here are the details:

> Transfer video to your Mac or PC from a VCR, DVR, camcorder, or any other analogue video device as a high-quality H.264 file. Elgato Video Capture is an easy-to-use software that assists you through every step, from connecting an analogue video device to capturing video and choosing how you will watch and share it.
>
> There is no easier way to digitize home video to playback on your computer, to sync with an iPad or iPhone, to edit in iMovie or Windows Live Movie Maker, or to upload to YouTube. The connection comes with Elgato Video Capture software for Mac and Windows.

(Cost approx. $85.)

Note that when using the Elgato Video Capture, you will need to have a video playback device, such as a VCR or MiniDV player, capable of playing your old-format recorded tapes.

38

Converting a Website or Video to a Static QR code on Your Computer

Throughout this book, I have used QR codes to allow you, while reading this book, to access and view videos, websites, and documents. These codes have become mainstream in our society and today are widely used. All you need is a mobile phone to scan the code, allowing you to view and/or store the embedded information.

There are two types of QR codes: static and dynamic. Static is used in this book; as their name implies, they cannot be changed. Dynamic codes often require an active subscription, and they *can* be changed. An example: ideal when the code is used to display a restaurant menu which gets regularly changed.

The best place to create codes is on your computer (you must incorporate a URL). I use this website to create my static QR codes: www.canva.com. An alternative site for creating QR codes is www.qrcode-tiger.com. Both offer subscriptions plus free usage.

The two most frequent uses for QR codes are websites and videos. The website URL is simply the website address (e.g., www.distinctivewalldecor.com).

I have included URLs along with most all QR codes in order to provide the reader with an alternative access to the websites and videos.

39

The Future of DIY Home-Improvement Retailing

There has been significant industry consolidation over the past several years. Today, Home Depot, Lowe's, Menards, and ACE Hardware remain the key drivers of this business in the USA.

Not long after Home Depot established itself as a dominant and powerful retail and contractor force, selling building material supplies, Lowe's, formally a nationwide chain of largely rural lumber and building material yards, was awakened!

They quickly regrouped and structured their stores—merchandising and product mix—to emulate that of Home Depot. Today in-store, the two companies look very much alike; the only real difference is that Home Depot's corporate color is orange, and Lowe's is blue. Both retailers have sales over $100 million, with Depot a little ahead of Lowe's. The current Lowe's CEO, Marvin Ellison, was, at one time, a senior executive working for Home Depot for about twelve years. In 2022, HD sales were $157 billion and Lowe's $97 billion.

Menards are also a significant component of the US DIY market. They are headquartered in Eau Claire, Wisconsin, founded and managed by John Menard, and remain a private company today.

Their stores are principally in the Midwest, in the northern half of the US. They differ from Home Depot and Lowe's in their merchandising presentation, having more decor focus and greater attention to the female customer.

These three chains overlap, particularly in the northern markets, where many trading areas have all three! John Menard is a hands-on leader and constantly challenges his two principal competitors.

ACE is a national chain of some five thousand independent hardware stores, owned and operated by local business entrepreneurs. They are well supported by a large and powerful Chicago headquarters merchandising and buying operation who provide to their members product sourcing and marketing support.

As a total retail organization, they command significant market clout and strength. While their product assortments do not match those of the three big-box retailers, previously discussed, they do have the capability of more personal customer product support and service in their stores.

40

The Future of Online Sales and Marketing

Back in the early days, when I was selling paint and wallcoverings, there was no such thing as online sales. If you wanted to buy a hammer, you drove to your nearby hardware or home center store. Selected the hammer, paid for it, and drove home. Nice and easy— but time-consuming!

Today you go to Amazon's website, or perhaps the website of one of the DIY retailers just discussed, and select the hammer of your choice, pay for it electronically with your credit card, and delivery will take place in a couple of days or so, directly to your home. Quick and easy!

The advantages of online buying are: time-saving, gasoline saving, often a wider assortment to select from, more opportunity to price shop—just easy!

So the question is—what's next? Perhaps by the time you have read the final chapter, there will be some new retail fulfillment option available that will dominate the procurement and supply of goods to homeowners worldwide!

EPILOGUE

At the conclusion of my memoir, I offer these thoughts, summarizing the key values.

I believe there is a defining moment in life that establishes your future course of events—positive or otherwise. In my case, it was my connecting with Mr. Dean Swift, the Sears regional president in the summer of 1968, during my early days as a salesman in Atlanta. Meeting with him and being exposed to and able to comprehend the monumental power and dominance of the Sears retail brand changed, for the better, the trajectory of my entire career. It inspired me to develop and expanded my sales and marketing horizon and skills in the years ahead.

This meeting also communicated to Glidden management my determination and goal to pursue a path of successful sales achievements. Aiming high, as I did on this occasion, will most often provide one with optimum results and opportunities—whatever the challenge may be. This single act of meeting with a Sears executive set me on a path that fueled my entire career.

The eighty-plus years of my journey have been packed with excitement, learning, hard work, much happiness, and a fair amount of success. I have been blessed with good health, a wonderful marriage, terrific children, and awesome grandchildren, who I hope may well follow and adopt some of my personal traits and characteristics.

The many friendships I have made along the way have been incredibly valuable and meaningful. I believe in the proverb "a friend in need, is a friend indeed." Today, one must work hard to develop and sustain long-term relationships, not just with friends and family but with every person you encounter, both in business and everyday life.

Integrity, honesty, and the respect for others should be a priority and a keystone in all our lives. So now remains the question, What's next? Writing this book is not a conclusion or a final act in my life but rather a pause to reflect on the past and share some of my ideas and experiences.

It's possible that I may write another book. This is my first. It really has been an enjoyable and satisfying experience writing, though a "second" would probably task my imagination as it may need to be a work of fiction!

This memoir is peppered with several how-to guides and solutions for various projects and activities. Hopefully, there is some value in this.

As recounted at the beginning, "loving my close-knit family has been the most fulfilling and happiest experience of my life," and "of all the accomplishments I have achieved in a lifetime, my family is what I am most proud of."

Writing a memoir, is no easy project—it tasks one's recollections fully and demands concise detail and a totally accurate recapitulation of events, dates, places, and names of all the included participants. I have strived to meet these standards.

Thank you for reading my story.

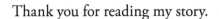

ACKNOWLEDGMENTS

I would like to express my special thanks and give credit to my publisher, the Covenant Books.

To my publication assistant, Rachel Cossentino, who worked closely with me, guiding the creation of my manuscript, and expertly counselled me through the entire process. She is professional, patient, and detail-oriented.

If you ever plan to write a book, be sure to contact her at rachel@covenantbooks.com.

APPENDIX 1

The Principal North American DIY Retailers – Both Past and Present

Note that some merchants are listed more than once, indicating their participation in several retail chain store operations.

Principals/buyers/merchants indicated are those I and my sales team directly met, communicated with, and sold to. Not all the names are included, and those shown are, in most all cases, not the current merchants.

AC Moore: Philadelphia, Pennsylvania; Tom Chisolm
ACE Hardware: Chicago, Illinois; Bill Smear, Alan Wucker
AllPro: Lansing, Michigan
Aikenheads: Toronto, Canada; Steve Bebis; purchased by THD in 1994, renamed THD Canada.
Ames
Associated Distributors/West Building Materials Atlanta: Bill Godwin, Charles West, Ed Plemons.
Ayrway: Indianapolis
Beaver Lumber: Toronto, Canada; Don Wilson; sold and rebranded in 2000
Beck & Gregg: Atlanta, Georgia; Wayne Pinson, Bobby Gilbert
Big K: Miami
Bradlees: Braintree, Massachusetts
Builder Marts of America: Columbia, South Carolina; Tom Mills
Builderama; Savannah; Jim Smith, Marvin Mednick

Builders Emporium: Irvine, California

Builders Square: San Antonio, Texas; Frank Denny, Frank Powers, Rob Lewis

Caldor: Port Chester, New York

Canadian Tire: Toronto, Canada; Ron Down

Chase Pitkin: Rochester, New York; Tim Machnick

Coast to Coast: Minneapolis, Minnesota; Ken Hoffman

Color Tile: Fort Worth, Texas; Larry Nagle, Eddie Lesok, Tom Dorman

Consumer Home Products: St. Louis, Missouri; Frank Ginsberg, Alan Hollander, Ted Berger

Copeland Lumber: Florence, Oregon

Cross Roads (Home Depot): Quincey, Illinois; Denny Ryan, Lenny Kapiloff, Jim Shalda

Daylin: Los Angeles, California; Dave Finkle, Sid Kline, Phyllis Freidman

Dixiline Hardware: Salana Beach, California; Jim Inglis, William Cowling; Builders First Source, Dallas, Texas

Do It Best

Dwoskin's: Atlanta, Georgia; Myron Dwoskin

Eaton: Toronto, Canada; Bill Prosser

Eclipse: St. Louis, Missouri; Steve Feinstein

Emery Waterhouse

Ernst: Seattle, Washington; Merrill Samuels, Doug Craig

Fed Mart: San Diego; Arnold Friedman

Federated Co-Op: Saskatoon, Canada; Bill Todd, Ken Faul

Forest City: Cleveland, Ohio; Max Rattner, Steve Feinstein, Bob Pliner, Lenny Filbin

Fred Meyer: Portland, Oregon; Jim Kief, Dave Wilson

Gold Circle: Columbus, Ohio; Bill Coleman, Ken Harris

Grossmans: Braintree, Massachusetts

Gulf Mart: San Antonio; Huey Stafford

Handy Andy: Chicago; Ron Raschow

Handy City: San Antonio; Joe Samulin, Huey Stafford

Handy Dan: San Diego, California; Frank Denny, John Markley, Joe Samulin

Handyman: San Diego, California; Herb Haimsohn, Bob Haimsohn
Hardware Sales & Service: Atlanta, Georgia; Bob Burdekin
Hechinger: Landover, Maryland
Hirshfields: Minneapolis, Minnesota; Ken Heidelburg
Homecrafters: Birmingham, Alabama; Cindy
Home Depot Expo: Barry Silverman
Home Depot: Atlanta; Bernie Marcus, Arthur Blank, Jim Inglis, Pat
    Farrah, Sophia Schade, Dennis Johnston, Steve Bebis
Home Quarters: Richmond, Virginia; Bob Shaw, Ben Mauceri
House Hasson: Nashville, Tennessee; Bill T
Hudsons: Detroit, Michigan
Inside Outlet
JCPenney: Plano, Texas
Jeffersons: Miami; Steve Danzig, Lyle Hartung
Kmart: Detroit, Michigan; Harry Hardisty; S. S. Kresge: Closed in
    1994
Linbrook Hardware: Santa Ana, California; Jerome Marks
Lindsley Lumber: Miami Springs, Florida; Paul Andert
Lockharts: Moncton, Canada; Jim Lockhart, Steve Valcour
Lowe's: Ross Burgiss, Walt McCall, Diane Eldridge
Lumber City: California
Meijer: Grand Rapids, Michigan; Harvey Lemmen, Harold Hans,
    Harvey Kooche, Ray Leach, Bob Barrett, Dwight Shupe
Menards: Eau Claire, Wisconsin; John Menard, Kelly Reese
Montgomery Ward: Chicago, Illinois; Mike Yergelovich
Moores: Virginia Beach, North Carolina; Bill Haynes
Mr. Goodbuys: Springfield, Pennsylvania
National Lumber: Los Angeles, California
National Merchandise: Jacksonville, Florida; A. R. Knight
New York Carpet: Detroit, Michigan; Marvin Berlin
Orgill: Memphis, Tennessee
Parade Stores: Minnesota
Pay'N Pak: John Markley
Pen Daniels: Quincy, Illinois
Pergament: New York, New York; Marty Pepkin
Plywood: Minnesota

Prange: Wisconsin; Roger Anderson
Revelstoke: Calgary, Canada
Richway: Atlanta; Ed Israel, Russell Waxman, Walt Sandlin
Rickel: South Plainfield, New Jersey
Roses: South Carolina; G. Dunn, Mark Steinberg
Scotty's: Winterhaven, Florida; Ray Cooney, Paul Blake
SE Nichols: New York, New York
Sears: Chicago, Illinois; Joe McGroarty, Bill Strauss, Fred Clackler
    (Atlanta), Jerry Post, Roger Benedict, Jean Benedict (carpet
    buyer), Dale Baccen, Sandy Rochliss
San Diego Glass & Paint: Robert Shipiro
Sherwin Williams, stores division: Cleveland, Ohio; Chris Connor,
    Wayne Kilbey, Gary Saiter, Bill Swinney, Steve Cunningham
Standard Brands: Torrance, California
Sutherland Lumber: Kansas City; Carl Iverson
Target: Minneapolis; Leroy Fish, Bill Miller
The Great Indoors: Chicago, Illinois
Venture: O'Fallon, Missouri; Jerry Emerick, John Belfi
Walmart: Bentonville, Arkansas; Joe Craig, Phil Lee
Wallpaper Atlanta: Tom Campbell
Wallpapers To Go: Los Angeles, California; Tracy Stevens, Jim
    Johnson
West Building Materials: Atlanta, Georgia; Charles West, John
    Breedlove, Bill Godwin
Wickes: Saginaw, Michigan; Walt McLellon, Dick Passaglia
Williams Brothers: Gainesville, Georgia; Harold Williams, Calvin
    Ballington
Woolco: New York
WT Grant: Dick Randall, Bill Ancona
Yardbirds: Petaluma, California (purchased by Home Depot; closed
    in 2009, along with HD Expo)

APPENDIX 2

USA & Canadian Leading Paint Manufacturers

Axalta Coatings: Glen Mills, Pennsylvania

AkzoNobel: Netherlands

Behr Process Corp: Santa Ana, California

Benjamin Moore: Montvale, New Jersey

Camco Paint: Tom Campbell (renamed Synta Paint; purchased by Rustoleum)

Glidden Paint: Cleveland, Ohio

ICI Paints: Slough, England (Dulux); Glidden: Cleveland, Ohio; Devoe, Fuller-O'Brien, Sinclair, C-I-L Paint, Color Your World, Liquid Nails.

Kelly-Moore Paint: San Carlos, California

Olympic Stain: Owned by PPG

PPG Industries: Pittsburgh, Pennsylvania

Pratt & Lambert

RPM International, Medina, Ohio

Sherwin Williams Paints, Valspar Paints: Cleveland, Ohio; Dutch Boy Paints, Krylon Aerosol Paints, Minwax, Thompson's, Cabot

Rustoleum: Chicago, Illinois

United Coatings: Chicago, Illinois (purchased by Pratt & Lambert)

Yenkin Majestic: Columbus, Ohio

APPENDIX 3

North American Sales

Graham & Brown and Home Depot Annual Sales
Graham & Brown (Solid Line) Currency: Millions (US dollar)
Home Depot (Dashes) Currency: Billions (US dollar)

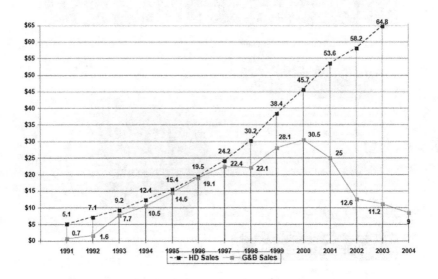

APPENDIX 4

Original Synta Deck Restore Press Release

NOT ALL ROLLER COVERS ARE THE SAME

Compare the Restore Roller™ to ordinary rollers and you will quickly see the difference. Both Deck Restore™ and Concrete Restore™ are thick coatings loaded with aggregates. The fibers of ordinary rollers entrap these aggregates in their nap creating an uneven, blotchy distribution of the coating. The Restore Roller™ leaves a slightly stippled coating on your surface.

The Restore Roller's™ open "honeycomb" weave absorbs the coating and releases just the right amount for the perfect application making the job much easier for the consumer or contractor.

AVAILABLE FALL 2009

ORDER INFORMATION:

Item Number – RRC-9-2009
UPC – 7-17650-92009-0
Packaging – One Roller cover per package.
Case Pack – 12
MSRP – $9.99
Shipping - FOB Clarkston, GA

 Synta, Inc., Clarkston, GA 30021 USA
1-800-373-6333
www.synta.com
Made in USA

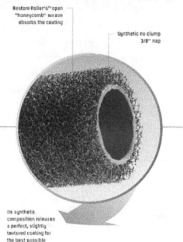

Restore Roller's™ open "honeycomb" weave absorbs the coating

Synthetic no clump 3/8" nap

Its synthetic composition releases a perfect, slightly textured coating for the best possible results

FEATURES:

- Delivers the best possible application
- 3/8" "honeycomb" nap
- Will not clog or clump
- Reuseable, easy clean up
- Fits standard rollers

<u>ORIGINAL SYNTA DECK RESTORE PRESS RELEASE</u>

SYNTA, INC. GIVES WOOD DECKS NEW LIFE WITH DECK RESTORE™

ATLANTA, GA (March 24, 2009) – SYNTA, INC announces the newest addition to its brand family. DECK RESTORE™ is a durable coating product formulated to resurface most wooden and composite decks, while providing lasting protection against moisture and the damaging effects of the sun. Designed for a variety of applications, it is the most cost effective and environmentally conscious way to revitalize wood surfaces.

DECK RESTORE™ can be applied over most outdoor wood surfaces to achieve a new finished look free of cracks and exposed splinters, often better than new! The coating is easily applied with a roller or brush and dries within hours to form a tough, resilient surface that will look beautiful and last for years for to come, with little maintenance. DECK RESTORE™ is slip resistant, flexible and chip-resistant even in cold weather. The tough film helps to resist blistering and peeling and recoats may extend the life of the system indefinitely

"Homeowners are looking for ways to improve their home while saving time and money," said Randy Moore, President, SYNTA, INC. We have delivered a quality product that will make older wood decks look like new, at a fraction of the cost of total surface replacement and have you ready to host your backyard barbecues in no time."

DECK RESTORE™ is currently being shipped to many National and Regional store locations.

About Synta
Synta is a prime paint manufacturer and contract packager serving global markets, wholesale and retail, for specialty architectural coatings, craft paints and industrial coatings.
All manufacturing, packaging and distribution operations are conveniently located in Clarkston Georgia with immediate access to Atlanta's perimeter highway.
Our mission is to consistently provide our customers products that deliver absolute satisfaction in appearance, application, and performance. We are dedicated to low cost, operational excellence that affords our customers the best opportunity to maximize sales and profits; always listening, always challenging, and always willing to change to better serve the customer.

ABOUT THE AUTHOR

Tony grew up in Birmingham, England, and attended Sebright boarding school in Wolverley, Worcestershire. Following graduation, he joined the Royal Warwickshire Regiment and was transferred to Malaya on active military service, joining the Sherwood Foresters Regiment. He was commissioned second lieutenant and, upon discharge, joined the Territorial Army Reserve and attained the rank of captain.

He worked for ICI paints division, where he held advertising and marketing positions at their Slough, England, headquarters, and later moved back to the Midlands as a sales representative.

On April 1, 1968, he immigrated to the United States, joined Glidden paints as a sales representative in Atlanta, Georgia. Two years later, he was transferred to their Cleveland, Ohio, headquarters to manage existing and sell to new retail chain account customers, throughout North America, as the National Account Manager. In 1972, he was promoted to Glidden's National Dealer Sales Manager in Cleveland.

In 1977, he was transferred to Glidden Toronto, where he managed their Canada-wide trade sales operation. Daughters: Heather was born in Cleveland on January 21, 1976, and Holly in Toronto on April 5, 1981. Both are wonderful, beautiful, and talented—happily married today, with incredible families.

Wishing to return to the United States, he resigned from Glidden; and together with his wife, Susan, and their two daughters, they moved to Atlanta, Georgia, on July 4, 1981. He founded and launched Horsley Marketing Services (HMS Inc.), a sales, marketing, and import business focused on DIY decorating products. This business successfully grew into a significant operation selling wallcoverings, imported from the UK to chain store operations throughout North America.

Upon retirement in 2006, along with his wife, they studied for and acquired a Realtor's license with Keller Williams. They enjoyed the business, particularly helping young buyers find and acquire their very first home. In 2009, Tony joined Synta Paint Company in Atlanta as a sales and marketing consultant to help them expand their business and customer base.

Gateway to America chronicles a busy, productive, and exciting life for the author and Susan, his wife of fifty years. It has been an incredible and fulfilling journey, and without question, their two daughters, both husbands, and seven grandchildren have added great joy, pride, and happiness to their lives.

Printed in the USA
CPSIA information can be obtained
at www.ICGtesting.com
LVHW020333211024
794345LV00009B/129